JANE'S POCKET BOOK OF

MILITARY TRANSPORT AND TRAINING AIRCRAFT

JANE'S POCKET BOOK OF

MILITARY TRANSPORT AND TRAINING AIRCRAFT

Compiled by MICHAEL J H TAYLOR and KENNETH MUNSON
Edited by JOHN W R TAYLOR FRHistS, AFRAeS, FSLAET

Collier Books
A Division of Macmillan Publishing Co., Inc.
New York

Macmillan Publishing Co., Inc.
866 Third Avenue, New York, N.Y. 10022
Collier-Macmillan Canada Ltd.

This edition is not available for sale in the United Kingdom and the British Commonwealth, except Canada

Library of Congress Catalog Card Number 73-15288

FIRST COLLIER BOOKS EDITION 1974

Also is published in a hardcover edition by

Macmillan Publishing Co., Inc.

PRINTED IN GREAT BRITAIN

FOREWORD

A modern air force is a highly complex service. Its first-line strength may be measured in terms of fighters, bombers, strike and anti-submarine aircraft; but it would have little practical value without a host of other types, of the kind described and illustrated in this Pocket Book.

Many times in the three decades that have followed the Second World War, military transport aircraft have demonstrated that they can prevent wars, or wage war, as effectively as the more aggressive categories of combat aircraft. As long ago as 1948-49, the freight-carrying transports of America, Britain and France averted a third World War by keeping West Berlin alive in the first great confrontation of the 'cold war' which we remember as the Berlin Air Lift.

At Suez and in Vietnam, the transports flew wingtip-to-wingtip with the fighters and bombers, air-dropping men and supplies, and performing entirely new tasks when fitted with electronic counter-measures equipment or heavy gunship armament. In Czechoslovakia in 1968, transport squadrons of the Soviet Air Force sent a shudder down the spines of Western strategists by demonstrating how quickly and efficiently they could set down an army of occupation, to smother a threatened rebellion, by night. There is little need to emphasise the part that sound training plays in such operations. But training aircraft, no less than transport aircraft and helicopters, are often adapted for more militant duties nowadays. Such a concept dates back at least as far as the Battle of Britain, when Tiger Moths and Harvards suddenly sprouted small bombs in defence of the United Kingdom. Today, some jet trainers can lift a weight of bombs, rockets, guns and other weapons that would not have disgraced a first-line bomber of 1940.

These are the kind of aircraft found in *Jane's Pocket Book of Military Transport and Training Aircraft.* Together with those in the *Pocket Book of Major Combat Aircraft* they give comprehensive, up-to-the-minute coverage of all major military aircraft in service or in production at the present time, in a compact, inexpensive form that is designed to appeal equally to professional users and the myriad enthusiasts and other readers who spot, build, fly, or simply want to know about the world's military aeroplanes and where they serve.

JWRT

Observation, light tactical support aircraft and general-purpose transport

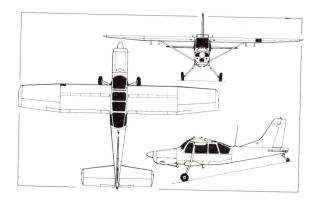

Power plant: One Piaggio-built Lycoming GSO-480-B1B6 six-cylinder piston engine (340 hp)
Wing span: 38 ft 6 in (11.73 m)
Length overall: 28 ft 8 in (8.73 m)
Cabin:
   Length 8 ft 2 in (2.50 m)
   Max width 2 ft 8 in (0.81 m)
   Max height 5 ft 3 in (1.60 m)
Normal T-O weight (2 crew only): 3 306 lb (1 500 kg)
Max T-O weight (with underwing weapons): 3 750 lb (1 700 kg)

AERITALIA AM3C (Italy)
First flight 1967

Max level speed at 8 000 ft (2 440 m), at normal T-O weight:
   150 knots (173 mph; 278 km/h)
Max rate of climb at S/L, normal T-O weight: 1 378 ft (420 m)/min
Service ceiling, normal T-O weight: 27 550 ft (8 400 m)
Max range at 5 000 ft (1 525 m), 30 min reserves, normal T-O weight: 534 nm (615 miles; 990 km)
Accommodation: Normally two persons in tandem, with dual controls. Provision at rear for two stretchers, a rear seat for one or two persons, or freight in place of this seat
Armament: Two underwing pylons standard, each able to carry up to 375 lb (170 kg) of stores, including a Matra pod containing two 7.62 mm machine-guns and 2 000 rounds of ammunition, a GE Minigun pod and 1 500 rounds, a Matra 125 pack of six 2.75 in rockets, a Matra 122 pack of seven BPD 50 mm rockets, a 113 kg GP bomb, an AN/M1A2 cluster of six 9 kg fragmentation bombs, an AN/M4A1 cluster of three 10 kg parachute-retarded fragmentation bombs, an M28A2 cluster of twenty-four 2 kg butterfly bombs, a Nord AS .11 or AS .12 wire-guided missile, an M84A1 target marker, an M46 photoflash or M26A1 parachute flare, or a 250 lb supply container. Alternatively, a Vinten 70 mm automatic three-camera reconnaissance pack can be carried under the fuselage; or two 70 mm cameras or a three-lens CA-103 camera inside the fuselage
Ordered by: Italy (Army 20), Rwanda (Air Force 3) and South Africa (Air Force 40)

Medium-range tactical transport

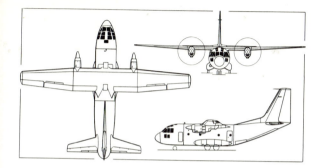

Wing span: 94 ft 6 in (28.80 m)
Length overall: 74 ft 5½ in (22.70 m)
Main cabin:
    Length 28 ft 1¾ in (8.58 m)
    Width 8 ft 0½ in (2.45 m)
    Height 7 ft 4½ in (2.25 m)
    Volume 1,660 cu ft (47.0 m³)
Max payload: 19 840 lb (9 000 kg)
Max T-O weight: 58 422 lb (26 500 kg)
Max level speed at 15 000 ft (4 575 m): 291 knots
(336 mph; 540 km/h)
Cruising speed at 14 750 ft (4 500 m): 194 knots (224
mph; 360 km/h)
Max rate of climb at S/L: 2 034 ft (620 m)/min
Service ceiling: 29 525 ft (9 000 m)
Basic mission range with 11 025 lb (5 000 kg)
payload: 1 591 nm (1 833 miles; 2 950 km)
Ferry range with max fuel: 2 670 nm (3 075 miles;
4 950 km)
Accommodation: Flight crew of three or four and up to
44 fully equipped troops or 32 paratroops. Alternative
payloads include 36 stretcher patients and eight
medical attendants or sitting casualties; or freight.
Typical Italian military equipment loads can include two
CL-52 light trucks, one CL-52 with a 105 mm L4
howitzer or one-ton trailer, Fiat AR-59 Campagnola
reconnaissance vehicle with 106 mm recoilless gun or
550 lb (250 kg) trailer, or five standard A-22 freight
containers
Ordered by: Italian Air Force (44)

Power plant: Two Fiat-built General Electric T64-P-4D
turboprop engines (each 3 400 shp)

9

NATO Code Name *Maya*
Basic and advanced trainer

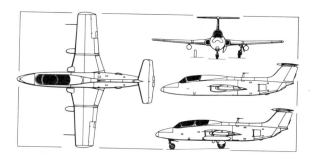

Drawing shows additional side view (centre) of single-seat
L-29A Akrobat

AERO L-29 DELFIN (Czechoslovakia)
First flight 1959

Data: Standard L-29
Power plant: One M 701c 500 turbojet engine (1 960
lb; 890 kg st)
Wing span: 33 ft 9 in (10.29 m)
Length overall: 35 ft 5½ in (10.81 m)
Normal T-O weight: 7 231 lb (3 280 kg)
Max permissible loaded weight with external tanks:
7 804 lb (3 540 kg)
**Max level speed at 16 400 ft (5 000 m), at AUW of
7 165 lb (3 250 kg):** 353 knots (407 mph; 655 km/h)
Max rate of climb at S/L, weight as above: 2 755 ft
(840 m)/min
Service ceiling, weight as above: 36 000 ft (11 000 m)
**Max range with external tanks at 16 400 ft (5 000 m),
weight as above:** 480 nm (555 miles; 894 km)
Accommodation: Crew of two in tandem on synchronised
ejection seats.

Armament: Provision for camera gun and gunsight, and
two bombs of up to 100 kg, eight air-to-ground rockets
or two 7.62 mm machine-gun pods under the wings
Ordered by: More than 3 000 built by early 1974, of
which more than 2 000 supplied to USSR for use as
trainers by the Soviet, Bulgarian, German (Democratic
Republic), Hungarian and Romanian air forces.
Remainder delivered to Czech Air Force or exported to
air forces of Egypt, Indonesia, Nigeria, Syria and
Uganda. Most of those exported to Africa and Middle
East are of the L-29R light attack version

Basic and advanced trainer (L-39) and light strike aircraft (L-39Z)

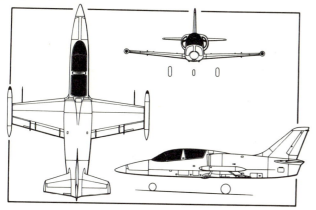

AERO L-39 (Czechoslovakia)
First flight 1968

Power plant: One Walter Titan (Motorlet-built Ivchenko AI-25W) turbofan engine (3 306 lb; 1 500 kg st)
Wing span: 29 ft 10¾ in (9.11 m)
Length overall: 39 ft 8¾ in (12.11 m)
Max T-O weight: 8 377 lb (3 800 kg)
Max level speed: 394 knots (454 mph; 730 km/h)
Max rate of climb at S/L: 3 740 ft (1 140 m)/min
Service ceiling: 37 225 ft (11 350 m)
Max range, tip-tanks full, no reserves: 805 nm (930 miles; 1 500 km)

Accommodation: Crew of two in tandem on zero-height ejection seats.
Armament: A prototype has flown with underwing rocket pods and air-to-air missiles, to evaluate its possible use as a light ground attack aircraft.
Ordered by: Pre-production batch of 10 built in 1971. Believed to have entered service in 1974 with Czech Air Force (L-39); L-39Z light attack version reportedly under development for Czechoslovakia and Iraq

AEROSPACE AIRTRAINER CT/4
(New Zealand)
First flight 1972

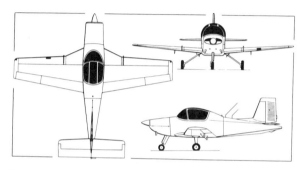

Data: Initial production version

Power plant: One Continental IO-360-D six-cylinder piston engine (210 hp) in prototype; optionally, one Lycoming IO-360-B four-cylinder piston engine (200 hp)

Wing span: 26 ft 0 in (7.92 m)

Length overall: 23 ft 2 in (7.06 m)

Cabin:

Length 9 ft 0 in (2.74 m)
Max width 3 ft 6½ in (1.08 m)
Max height 4 ft 5 in (1.35 m)

Max T-O weight: 2 350 lb (1 066 kg)

Max level speed at 10 000 ft (3 050 m), prototype with 210 hp engine: 146 knots (168 mph; 270 km/h)

Cruising speed at 10 000 ft (3 050 m), 75% power, prototype with 210 hp engine: 125 knots (144 mph; 232 km/h)

Max rate of climb at S/L, prototype with 210 hp engine: 1 350 ft (411 m)/min

Service ceiling, prototype with 210 hp engine: 17 900 ft (5 455 m)

Max range at S/L at 102.5 knots (118 mph; 190 km/h), prototype with 210 hp engine: 767 nm (884 miles; 1 422 km)

Range with 10% reserves, prototype with 210 hp engine and no tip-tanks:

75% power at S/L 581 nm (669 miles; 1 076 km)
75% power at 5 000 ft (1 525 m) 670 nm (772 miles; 1 242 km)
55% power at S/L 660 nm (760 miles; 1 223 km)
65% power at 5 000 ft (1 525 m) 716 nm (825 miles; 1 327 km)

Accommodation: Two seats side by side, and dual controls. Space at rear for optional third seat or 115 lb (52 kg) of baggage or equipment

Ordered by: Air forces of Australia (37) and Thailand (24)

General-purpose helicopters

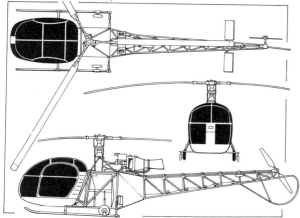

Photo and drawing: Alouette II

Data: SA 315B Lama (known as Cheetah in India)

Power plant: One Turboméca Artouste IIIB turboshaft engine (870 shp, derated to 550 shp)

Main rotor diameter: 36 ft 1¾ in (11.02 m)

Length overall, both rotors turning: 42 ft 4¾ in (12.92 m)

Max T-O weight with externally-slung cargo: 4 850 lb (2 200 kg)

Max cruising speed with slung load: 65 knots (75 mph; 120 km/h)

AÉROSPATIALE ALOUETTE II and LAMA (France)
First flights 1955/1969

Max rate of climb at S/L with slung load: 820 ft (250 m)/min

Service ceiling with slung load: 13 125 ft (4 000 m)

Accommodation: Pilot and passenger side by side in front, and three passengers behind. Provision for external sling loads of up to 2 204 lb (1 000 kg). Can be equipped for rescue, liaison, observation, training, agricultural, photographic, ambulance and other duties. Ambulance accommodates two stretchers and a medical attendant internally

Ordered by: Air forces of Austria (16 Artouste-engined Alouette), Belgium (Army/Police 39 Artouste, 67 Astazou-engined Alouette), Cameroun (1 Alouette), Central African Republic (1 Artouste), Chad (1 Artouste), Congo (1 Artouste), Dominica (2 Artouste), Finland (1 Astazou), France (Air Force/Navy/Army 363 Artouste, Army 15 Astazou), German Federal Republic (Air Force/Army 338 Alouette), Gabon (3 Alouette), India (Navy 2 Alouette, Army 140 Lama/Cheetah), Indonesia (3 Artouste), Israel (5 Artouste), Ivory Coast (2 Artouste), Jamaica (2 Alouette), Kenya (3 Alouette), Khmer (8 Artouste), Laos (2 Artouste), Lebanon (4 Artouste), Libya (3 Alouette), Malagasy (1 Astazou), Mexico (7 Alouette), Morocco (7 Artouste), Nigeria (2 Astazou), Peru (6 Artouste), Portugal (7 Artouste), Senegal (2 Astazou), South Africa (7 Artouste), Sweden (Air Force/Navy/Army 25 Artouste), Switzerland (30 Artouste), Togo (1 Alouette), Tunisia (8 Artouste), UK (Army 17 Artouste), Venezuela (1 Alouette), South Vietnam (2 Astazou) and Zaïre (5 Alouette)

Advanced trainer and light attack aircraft

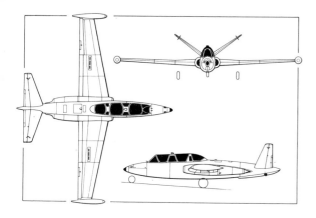

Wing span over tip-tanks: 39 ft 10 in (12.15 m)
Length overall: 33 ft 0 in (10.06 m)
Max T-O weight: 7 187 lb (3 260 kg)
Max level speed at 30 000 ft (9 000 m): 392 knots
(451 mph; 725 km/h)
Max rate of climb at S/L:
  at 2 850 kg AUW 3 935 ft (1 200 m)/min
  at 3 100 kg AUW 3 740 ft (1 140 m)/min
Service ceiling at 3 100 kg AUW: 39 375 ft (12 000 m)
**Range at 30 000 ft (9 000 m) with 26 Imp gallons
(120 litres) fuel reserve:**
  at 2 850 kg AUW 490 nm (565 miles; 910 km)
  at 3 100 kg AUW 755 nm (870 miles; 1 400 km)
Armament: Two 7.5 or 7.62 mm machine-guns (200
rds/gun) in fuselage nose. Gyro gunsight in each
cockpit, that in rear cockpit fitted with additional peris-
copic sight. Racks may be fitted under each wing for
two 25 kg air-to-ground rockets, one Matra 181
launcher with eighteen 37 mm rockets, one launcher
with seven 68 mm rockets, one 50 kg bomb or one
Nord AS.11 guided missile
Ordered by: Air forces of Algeria (28), Austria (18),
Belgium (approx 30), Brazil (7), Finland (82), France
(Air Force 400, Navy 30 carrier-equipped Zephyr),
German Federal Republic (250), Israel (52), Khmer (4),
Lebanon (4), Libya (20), Morocco (8), Uganda (12) and
Zaire (6)

Photo and drawing: CM 170 Magister
Data: Super Magister
Power plant: Two Turboméca Marboré VI turbojet en-
gines (each 1 058 lb; 480 kg st)

Aircrew trainer and light transport

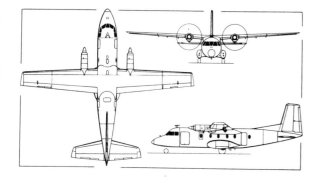

Data: Frégate Series D

Power plant: Two Turboméca Bastan VII turboprop engines (each 1 145 ehp)

Wing span: 74 ft 1¾ in (22.60 m)

Length overall: 63 ft 3 in (19.28 m)

Cabin, including baggage space and toilet:
Length 34 ft 10 in (10.61 m)
Max width 7 ft 1 in (2.15 m)
Max height 5 ft 11 in (1.80 m)
Volume 1 146 cu ft (32.5 m³)

Max payload: 6 779 lb (3 075 kg)

Max T-O weight: 23 810 lb (10 800 kg)

Max and econ cruising speed: 220 knots (254 mph; 408 km/h)

Max rate of climb at S/L: 1 380 ft (420 m)/min

Service ceiling: 28 500 ft (8 690 m)

Range with max fuel, no reserves: 1 295 nm (1 490 miles; 2 400 km)

Accommodation: Flight crew of two and up to 29 passengers. Movable forward bulkhead to cater for variable mixed cargo/passenger layouts. Army versions can be fitted out to carry 18 paratroops or 29 troops, or as a 22-seat transport. Naval versions (N 262 Series A) can be fitted out for target towing, artillery and missile observation, radar calibration or crew training duties. The Frégate Series D aircraft of the French Air Force are for training and liaison duties

Ordered by: France (Air Force 6 N 262 Srs A, of which 5 since transferred to Navy, and 18 Frégate Srs D; Navy 16 N 262 Srs A)

Photo and drawing: Frégate Series D

21

General-purpose helicopter

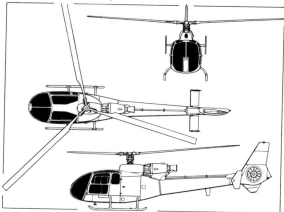

Data: Initial production version
Power plant: One Turboméca Astazou III turboshaft engine (590 shp)
Main rotor diameter: 34 ft 5½ in (10.50 m)
Length overall: 39 ft 3⁵⁄₁₆ in (11.97 m)
Cabin:
Length 7 ft 2⁹⁄₁₆ in (2.20 m)
Max width 4 ft 4 in (1.32 m)
Max height 3 ft 11⅝ in (1.21 m)
Volume 63.7 cu ft (1.80 m³)
Baggage hold volume 15.9 cu ft (0.45 m³)

AÉROSPATIALE/WESTLAND SA 341
GAZELLE (France/UK)
First flight 1967

Max T-O weight: 3 970 lb (1 800 kg)
Max cruising speed at S/L: 142 knots (164 mph; 264 km/h)
Max rate of climb at S/L: 1 770 ft (540 m)/min
Service ceiling: 16 400 ft (5 000 m)
Range at S/L with max fuel: 361 nm (416 miles; 670 km)
Accommodation: Pilot and second pilot or passenger side by side in front and three passengers behind. Rear bench seat can be folded into floor wells to leave a completely flat cargo floor. Baggage compartment at rear of cabin
Armament: Military loads can include two pods of 36 mm rockets, four AS.11 or Hot wire-guided missiles or two AS.12s with APX-Bézu 334 gyro-stabilised sight, four TOW missiles with XM 26 sight, two forward-firing 7.62 mm machine-guns, reconnaissance flares or smoke markers, cabin-mounted side-firing GE Minigun or 7.62 mm machine-gun or Emerson Minitat or chin turret mounting with pantograph sight system
Ordered by: France (Army 166 SA 341F) and UK (Air Force 13 SA 341D/HT. Mk 3 and SA 341E/HCC. Mk 4, Navy 30 SA 341C/HT. Mk 2, Army/Royal Marines 99 SA 341B/AH. Mk 1). Military export version is SA 341H, civil version is SA 341G. Also manufactured under licence in Yugoslavia

Primary trainer

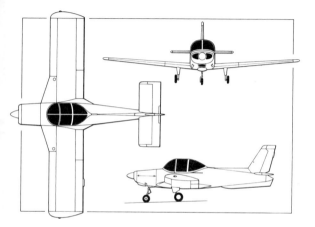

Data: Standard T-23 military version
Power plant: One Lycoming 0-320-B2B four-cylinder
   piston engine (160 hp)
Wing span: 27 ft 10¾ in (8.50 m)
Length overall: 21 ft 8 in (6.60 m)
Max T-O weight: 1 825 lb (840 kg)
Max level speed: 122 knots (140 mph; 225 km/h)
Max cruising speed at 5 000 ft (1 525 m): 100 knots
   (115 mph; 185 km/h)
Max rate of climb at S/L: 787 ft (240 m)/min
Service ceiling: 14 760 ft (4 500 m)
Max range: 429 nm (495 miles; 800 km)
Accommodation: Two seats side by side, with dual con-
   trols. Baggage compartment, capacity 66 lb (30 kg), aft
   of seats
Ordered by: Air forces of Brazil (70) and Paraguay (20)

NATO Code Name *Cub*
Medium/long-range freight and troop transport

ANTONOV An-12 (USSR)
First flight 1959 (?)

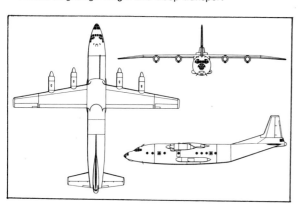

Data: Standard military version

Power plant: Four Ivchenko AI-20K turboprop engines (each 4 000 ehp)

Wing span: 124 ft 8 in (38.00 m)

Length overall: 121 ft 4½ in (37.00 m)

Cargo hold:
Length 44 ft 3½ in (13.50 m)
Max width 9 ft 10 in (3.00 m)
Max height 7 ft 10½ in (2.40 m)

Max civil payload: 44 090 lb (20 000 kg)

Normal T-O weight: 121 475 lb (55 100 kg)

Max level speed: 419 knots (482 mph; 777 km/h)

Max cruising speed: 361 knots (416 mph; 670 km/h)

Max rate of climb at S/L: 1 970 ft (600 m)/min

Service ceiling: 33 500 ft (10 200 m)

Range with max payload: 1 942 nm (2 236 miles; 3 600 km)

Range with max fuel: 3 075 nm (3 540 miles; 5 700 km)

Accommodation: Flight crew of five plus a rear gunner in tail turret. Primary role is that of cargo transport, but aircraft can accommodate 100 paratroops, all of whom can be despatched in under one minute

Armament: Two 23 mm NR-23 cannon in tail turret

Ordered by: Air forces of Algeria (8), Egypt (20), India (34), Indonesia (10), Iraq (8), Poland and USSR; all quantities estimated

NATO Code Name *Clod*
Light general-purpose transport

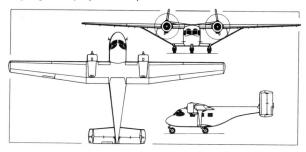

Data: Standard production An-14
Power plant: Two Ivchenko AI-14RF nine-cylinder radial piston engines (each 300 hp)
Wing span: 72 ft 2 in (21.99 m)
Length overall: 37 ft 6½ in (11.44 m)

ANTONOV An-14 PCHELKA (USSR)
First flight 1958

Cabin, excluding flight deck:
Length 10 ft 2 in (3.10 m)
Width 5 ft 0 in (1.53 m)
Height 5 ft 3 in (1.60 m)
Max payload (normal): 1 590 lb (720 kg)
Max T-O weight: 7 935 lb (3 600 kg)
Max level speed at 3 280 ft (1 000 m): 120 knots (138 mph; 222 km/h)
Normal cruising speed at 6 560 ft (2 000 m): 97 knots (112 mph; 180 km/h)
Max rate of climb at S/L: 1 000 ft (306 m)/min
Service ceiling: 17 060 ft (5 200 m)
Range:
with max payload 350 nm (404 miles; 650 km)
with 1 212 lb (550 kg) payload 385 nm (444 miles; 715 km)
with max fuel 431 nm (497 miles; 800 km)
Accommodation: Pilot and one passenger side by side on flight deck, and up to seven passengers in main cabin. All seats quickly removable to provide an unobstructed cabin for cargo carrying. Ambulance version can accommodate six stretchers and an attendant. Dual controls available for pilot training
Ordered by: Air forces of German Democratic Republic, Guinea and USSR. Prototype flown in 1969 of An-28, an enlarged version with 810 shp Isotov TVD-850 turboprop engines and accommodation for up to 15 persons or equivalent freight; this version not known to have entered service by early 1974

NATO Code Name *Cock*
Long-range strategic heavy transport

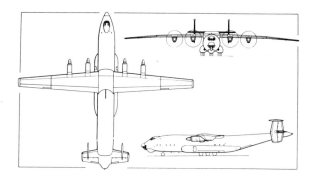

ANTONOV An-22 ANTHEUS (USSR)
First flight 1965

Data: Current production version
Power plant: Four Kuznetsov NK-12MA turboprop engines (each 15 000 shp)
Wing span: 211 ft 4 in (64.40 m)
Length overall (prototype): 189 ft 7 in (57.80 m)
Main cabin:
    Length 108 ft 3 in (33.00 m)
    Max width 14 ft 5 in (4.40 m)
    Max height 14 ft 5 in (4.40 m)
Max payload: 176 350 lb (80 000 kg)
Max T-O weight: 551 160 lb (250 000 kg)
Max level speed: 399 knots (460 mph; 740 km/h)
Range with max fuel and 99 200 lb (45 000 kg) payload: 5 905 nm (6 800 miles; 10 950 km)
Range with max payload: 2 692 nm (3 100 miles; 5 000 km)
Accommodation: Crew of five or six. Navigator's station in nose. Cabin for 28-29 passengers aft of flight deck, separated from main cabin by a bulkhead. Uninterrupted main cabin for freight
Ordered by: Soviet Air Force

NATO Code Names *Coke* and *Curl*
Short-range troop and vehicle transports

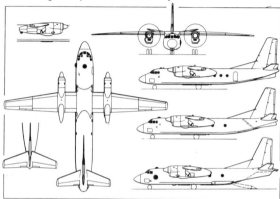

Photo: An-24V Srs 11 **Data:** An-26

Drawing: An-26. An-24T side view (centre). An-24V side view (top) and tail (left)

Power plant: Two Ivchenko AI-24T turboprop engines (each 2 820 ehp); one RU 19-300 auxiliary turbojet (1 985 lb; 900 kg st) in starboard nacelle for use, as required, at T-O, during climb and in level flight, and for self-contained starting of main engines

Wing span: 95 ft 9½ in (29.20 m)

Length overall: 78 ft 1 in (23.80 m)

Cargo hold:
Length of floor 37 ft 8¾ in (11.50 m)

ANTONOV An-24 and An-26 (USSR)
First flights 1960/1968 (?)

Width of floor 7 ft 10½ in (2.40 m)
Max height 6 ft 3 in (1.91 m)

Max payload: 12 125 lb (5 500 kg)

Normal T-O weight: 50 706 lb (23 000 kg)

Max T-O weight: 52 911 lb (24 000 kg)

Cruising speed at 19 675 ft (6 000 m), at normal T-O weight: 229-234 knots (264-270 mph; 425-435 km/h)

Max rate of climb at S/L, at normal T-O weight: 1 575 ft (480 m)/min

Service ceiling, at normal T-O weight: 24 600 ft (7 500 m)

Range, with allowance for taxying and 1 278 lb (580 kg) reserve fuel, at normal T-O weight:
with 9 920 lb (4 500 kg) payload 485 nm (559 miles; 900 km)
with 4 687 lb (2 126 kg) payload 1 214 nm (1 398 miles; 2 250 km)

Accommodation: Flight crew of five, plus freight. Can accommodate a variety of motor vehicles, including GAZ-69 and UAZ-469 military vehicles, or cargo items up to 59 in (1.50 m) high by 82.6 in (2.10 m) wide. Cabin fitted with a row of tip-up seats along each wall to accommodate up to 40 paratroops. Conversion to troop transport role, or to ambulance for 24 stretcher patients and a medical attendant, takes 20-30 min.

Ordered by: Air forces of Congo (2), Czechoslovakia (2), Egypt (3), German Democratic Republic, North Korea, Mongolia, Romania (4), Somalia (1), USSR and North Vietnam (4) have An-24; Soviet Air Force believed to have An-26. All quantities estimated

Carrier-based fighter

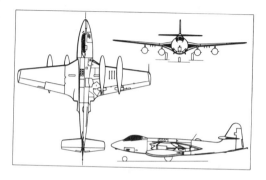

Drawing: Sea Hawk Mk 100

ARMSTRONG WHITWORTH SEA HAWK
(UK)
First flight 1947

Data: F (GA). Mk 6
Power plant: One Rolls-Royce Nene 103 turbojet engine (5 400 lb; 2 450 kg st)
Wing span: 39 ft 0 in (11.89 m)
Length overall: 39 ft 8 in (12.09 m)
Max T-O weight: 16 200 lb (7 348 kg)
Max level speed at S/L, at 13 600 lb (6 170 kg) AUW: 520 knots (599 mph; 964 km/h)
Combat radius at above AUW: 200 nm (230 miles; 370 km)
Combat radius with two 100 Imp gallon (455 litre) drop-tanks, at above AUW: 335 nm (386 miles; 621 km)
Armament: Four 20 mm cannon mounted in lower portion of fuselage nose. Provision for carrying bombs, rockets or a Sidewinder air-to-air missile under each wing
Ordered by: Indian Navy (24 FGA. Mk 6, 22 ex-RN FGA. Mks 4/6 and 28 ex-German Mks 100/101, of which approx 30 still in service 1974)

Long-range troop and freight transport

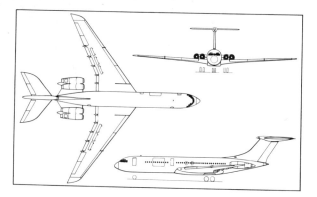

BAC VC10 (UK)
First flight 1962

Photo, drawing and data: C.Mk.1 (Model 1106)
Power plant: Four Rolls-Royce Conway RCo.43 Mk 301
   turbofan engines (each 21 800 lb; 9 888 kg st)
Wing span: 146 ft 2 in (44.55 m)
Length overall: 158 ft 8 in (48.36 m)
Cabin, excluding flight deck:
   Length 92 ft 4 in (28.14 m)
   Max width 11 ft 6 in (3.50 m)
   Max height 7 ft 5 in (2.26 m)
   Volume 6 700 cu ft (189.7 m³)
Freight holds:
   fwd 615 cu ft (17.40 m³)
   rear 797 cu ft (22.56 m³)
Max payload: 57 400 lb (26 030 kg)
Max T-O weight: 323 000 lb (146 510 kg)
Max cruising speed at 31 000 ft (9 450 m): 504 knots
   (581 mph; 935 km/h)
Max rate of climb at S/L: 3 050 ft (930 m)/min
**Range with max payload, cruising at 369 knots
(425 mph; 683 km/h) at 30 000 ft (9 145 m):**
3 385 nm (3 900 miles; 6 275 km)
Accommodation: Flight crew of four and up to 150
passengers or 76 stretchers and 6 medical attendants.
Two underfloor freight holds, one at front and one at
rear
Ordered by: Royal Air Force (14)

BEAGLE BASSET (UK)
First flight 1964

Data: Basset CC.Mk 1
Power plant: Two Rolls-Royce Continental GIO-470-A six-cylinder piston engines (each 310 hp)
Wing span: 45 ft 9½ in (13.96 m)
Length overall: 33 ft 3 in (10.13 m)
Cabin:
    Length 11 ft 11 in (3.63 m)
    Max width 5 ft 2 in (1.57 m)
    Max height 4 ft 4 in (1.32 m)
    Volume 196.5 cu ft (5.56 m³)
Max payload, excluding pilot, radio, oil and fuel: 1 800 lb (816 kg)
Max T-O weight: 7 500 lb (3 402 kg)
Max level speed at 8 000 ft (2 440 m) at 7 300 lb (3 311 kg) AUW: 182 knots (210 mph; 338 km/h)
Max rate of climb at S/L: 1 170 ft (357 m)/min
Service ceiling at AUW of 7 000 lb (3 175 kg): 17 500 ft (5 330 m)
Range with max fuel, no allowances: 1 565 nm (1 805 miles; 2 900 km)
Range with 1 500 lb (680 kg) payload: 442 nm (509 miles; 809 km)
Range with 950 lb (431 kg) payload: 1 020 nm (1 175 miles; 1 891 km)
Accommodation: Standard seating for five to eight persons, including pilot. Rear seats can be removed for cargo-carrying
Ordered by: Air forces of Syria (1 similar Beagle B.206) and UK (20 Basset)

Basic and intermediate trainer

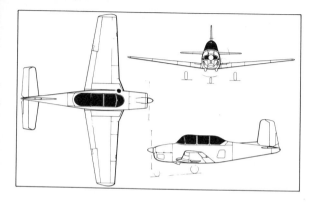

Photo and drawing: T-34B Mentor

BEECHCRAFT T-34 MENTOR and FUJI LM-1/LM-2 NIKKO /KM-2 (USA/Japan)
First flights 1948/1955/1962

Data: Fuji KM-2
Power plant: One Lycoming IGSO-480-A1F6 six-cylinder piston engine (340 hp)
Wing span: 32 ft 10 in (10.00 m)
Length overall: 26 ft 0¾ in (7.94 m)
Cabin:
Length 10 ft 2 in (3.10 m)
Max width 3 ft 6 in (1.07 m)
Max height 4 ft 1 in (1.24 m)
Max T-O weight: 3 860 lb (1 750 kg)
Max level speed at 16 000 ft (4 880 m): 200 knots (230 mph; 370 km/h)
Max rate of climb at S/L: 1 160 ft (354 m)/min
Service ceiling: 24 000 ft (7 310 m)
Range with standard fuel: 495 nm (570 miles; 915 km)
Accommodation: Seating for two or four persons. Dual controls standard
Ordered by: Air forces of Argentine (75), Chile (66), Colombia (41), Ecuador, El Salvador (3), Indonesia (40 Fuji T-34), Japan (Air Force 140 Fuji T-34; Navy 28 KM-2; Army 27 LM-1, of which 2 cvtd to LM-2), Mexico (Navy 4), Philippines (36 Fuji T-34), Spain (25), Turkey (24), Uruguay (Navy 1) and Venezuela (34)

Light transport (Baron) and instrument trainer (Cochise)

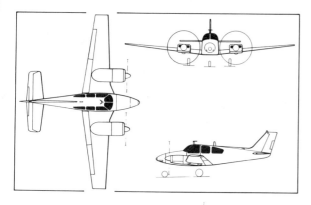

BEECHCRAFT T-42A COCHISE and BARON (USA)
First flights 1960/1965

Data: Model B55 Baron (T-42A similar)
Power plant: Two Continental IO-470-L six-cylinder piston engines (each 260 hp)
Wing span: 37 ft 10 in (11.53 m)
Length overall: 27 ft 0 in (8.23 m)
Cabin:
Length 8 ft 6 in (2.59 m)
Max width 3 ft 6 in (1.07 m)
Max height 4 ft 2 in (1.27 m)
Baggage compartments:
fwd 12 cu ft (0.34 m³)
rear 35 cu ft (0.99 m³)
Max T-O weight: 5 100 lb (2 313 kg)
Max level speed at S/L: 205 knots (236 mph: 380 km/h)
Max rate of climb at S/L: 1 670 ft (510 m)/min
Service ceiling: 19 700 ft (6 000 m)
Range with 45% power at 12 000 ft (3 660 m) with max fuel, allowances for warm-up, T-O, climb, and 45 min fuel reserve: 1 057 nm (1 218 miles; 1 960 km)
Accommodation: Seating for between four and six persons, including pilot
Ordered by: Air forces of Peru (T-42A), Rhodesia (1 Baron), Spain (7 B55 Baron), Turkey (Army 5 T-42A) and USA (Army 65 T-42A)

Light transport and navigation trainer

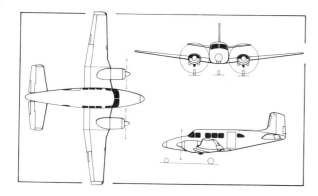

Photo and drawing: U-8F Seminole
Data: U-8F
Power plant: Two Lycoming IGSO-480-A1B6 six-cylinder piston engines (each 340 hp)

BEECHCRAFT U-8 SEMINOLE (USA)
First flight 1952

Wing span: 45 ft 10½ in (13.98 m)
Length overall: 35 ft 6 in (10.82 m)
Cabin:
Length 9 ft 4 in (2.84 m)
Max width 4 ft 6 in (1.37 m)
Max height 4 ft 9 in (1.45 m)
Volume 199.5 cu ft (5.65 m³)

Baggage compartment: 42 cu ft (1.19 m³)
Max T-O weight: 7 700 lb (3 493 kg)
Max level speed at 12 000 ft (3 600 m): 208 knots (239 mph; 384 km/h)
Cruising speed (70% power) at 15 200 ft (4 630 m): 186 knots (214 mph; 344 km/h)
Max rate of climb at S/L: 1 300 ft (396 m)/min
Service ceiling at 6 500 lb (2 950 kg) AUW: 31 300 ft (9 540 m)
Range with max fuel at 149 knots (171 mph; 275 km/h), 45 min reserves: 1 059 nm (1 220 miles; 1 963 km)
Accommodation: Seating for six persons including crew of one or two
Ordered by: Air forces of Japan (Navy 29 similar Queen Air 65), Morocco (2 similar Twin-Bonanza), Pakistan (1 Twin-Bonanza), Peru (21 Queen Air 65 & 80), Switzerland (3 Twin-Bonanza), Uruguay (Queen Air 65), USA (Army 170 U-8D and 8 RU-8D, incl 93 cvtd from L-23A/B, approx 12 more RU-8D, 6 U-8E and 71 U-8F; some RU-8D/U-8E cvtd to U-8G) and Venezuela (6 Queen Air 65)

General-purpose transport and surveillance aircraft

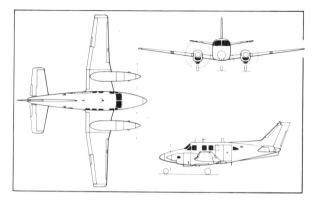

Photo: RU-21E
Drawing: U-21A

BEECHCRAFT U-21 (USA)
First flight 1964

Data: U-21F
Power plant: Two Pratt and Whitney (UACL) PT6A-28 turboprop engines (each 680 ehp)
Wing span: 45 ft 10½ in (13.98 m)
Length overall: 39 ft 8½ in (12.10 m)
Max T-O weight: 11 500 lb (5 216 kg)
Max cruising speed at 10 000 ft (3 050 m) at 10 500 lb (4 762 kg) AUW: 248 knots (285 mph; 459 km/h)
Max rate of climb at S/L: 1 963 ft (598 m)/min
Service ceiling: 24 850 ft (7 575 m)
Range, at high cruise power, with 470 US gallons (1 779 litres) fuel, includes allowances for starting, taxi, T-O, climb, descent and 45 min reserve, at 21 000 ft (6 400 m): 1 212 nm (1 395 miles; 2 245 km)
Accommodation: Flight crew of two, with dual controls, and up to 13 passengers, plus up to 410 lb (186 kg) of baggage in aft fuselage
Ordered by: USA (Air Force 1 VC-6A; Army 121 U-21A, 3 JU-21A, 4 RU-21A, 3 RU-21B, 2 RU-21C, 18 RU-21D, 16 RU-21E, and 8 U-21F which include 3 Super King Air 200)

Armed light observation (Bell 206/OH-58) and primary training (TH-57A) helicopter

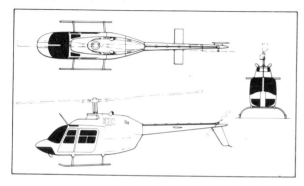

Photo and drawing: OH-58A Kiowa

Data: OH-58A
Power plant: One Allison T63-A-700 turboshaft engine (317 shp)
Main rotor diameter: 35 ft 4 in (10.77 m)
Length of fuselage: 32 ft 7 in (9.93 m)
Max T-O weight: 3 000 lb (1 360 kg)
Max permissible speed at S/L, estimated at observation mission gross weight of 2 768 lb (1 255 kg): 120 knots (138 mph; 222 km/h)
Cruising speed for max range, weight as above: 102 knots (117 mph; 188 km/h)

BELL 206/OH-58A KIOWA/TH-57A SEARANGER (USA)
First flights 1966/1968/1968

Max rate of climb at S/L, weight as above: 1 780 ft (543 m)/min
Service ceiling, weight as above: 18 900 ft (5 760 m)
Max range at S/L, 10% reserves, weight as above: 259 nm (299 miles; 481 km)
Max range at S/L, armed scout mission at max T-O weight, no reserves: 264 nm (305 miles; 490 km)
Accommodation: Forward crew compartment seats pilot and co-pilot/observer side by side. Cargo/passenger compartment provides approx 40 cu ft (1.13 m³) of cargo area, or provisions for two passengers
Armament: Standard equipment is the XM-27 armament kit, utilising the 7.62 mm Minigun. Some Brazilian Air Force OH-4s have a four-tube M2A2 launcher for 2.75 in rockets, mounted at the aft edge of the port door, and a 0.50 in machine-gun on a flexible mount by the starboard door
Ordered by: Air forces of Australia (Navy 9 206B-1, Army 75 206B-1), Austria (13 AB 206A), Brazil (7 OH-4, incl 4 armed for COIN duties), Brunei (Army 4 206A), Canada (Armed Forces 74 COH-58A), Iran (70 AB 206A), Italy (armed forces 84 AB 206A/A-1), Jamaica (Defence Force 1 206A), Libya (2 AB 206A), Oman (4 AB 206A), Saudi Arabia (24 AB 206A), Spain (Army 22 AB 206A/OH-58A), Sri Lanka (9 206A), Sweden (Navy 10 AB 206A, Army 44 AB 206A), Turkey (Army 50 AB 206A) and USA (Navy 40 TH-57A SeaRanger, Army 2,200 OH-58A Kiowa)

Strategic (C-135) and VIP (VC-137/707) transport

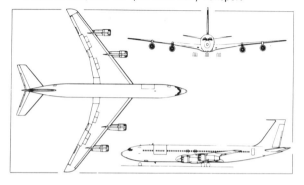

Photo and drawing: CC-137 (707-320C)

BOEING C-135/VC-137/707 (USA)
First flights 1961/1958/1954

Data: VC-137C
Power plant: Four Pratt and Whitney JT3D-3 turbofan engines (each 18 000 lb; 8 165 kg st)
Wing span: 145 ft 9 in (44.42 m)
Length overall: 152 ft 11 in (46.61 m)
Cabin, excl flight deck:
  Length 111 ft 6 in (33.99 m)
  Max width 11 ft 8 in (3.55 m)
  Max height 7 ft 7 in (2.31 m)
  Volume 7 983 cu ft (226 m³)
Max payload: 53 300 lb (24 175 kg)
Max T-O weight: 328 000 lb (148 778 kg)
Econ cruising speed: 478 knots (550 mph; 886 km/h)
Max rate of climb at S/L: 3 550 ft (1 082 m)/min
Service ceiling: 38 500 ft (11 735 m)
Range with max fuel: 6 080 nm (7 000 miles; 11 265 km)
Accommodation: Crew of seven or eight, and up to 49 VIP passengers.
Ordered by: Air forces of Canada (5 CC-137/707-347C), German Federal Republic (4 707-307C), Portugal (3 707-3F5C), Taiwan (1 720-047B) and USA (18 C-135A; 30 C-135B of which 11 cvtd to VC-135B and 10 to WC-135B; 3 VC-137A/B:707-153B; and 2 VC-137C:707-353B). See Pocketbook No 2 for tanker, airborne command post and special reconnaissance versions

Navigation trainer (T-43A) and short-range transport (737)

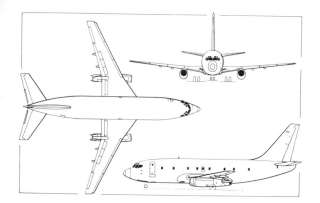

Data: T-43A
Power plant: Two Pratt and Whitney JT8D-9 turbofan engines (each 14 500 lb; 6 575 kg st)
Wing span: 93 ft 0 in (28.35 m)
Length overall: 100 ft 0 in (30.48 m)
Cabin (737-200), incl galley and toilet:
  Length 68 ft 6 in (20.88 m)
  Max width 11 ft 6½ in (3.52 m)
  Max height 7 ft 2 in (2.18 m)
  Volume 4 636 cu ft (131.28 m³)
Max payload: 35 700 lb (16 193 kg)
Max T-O weight: 115 500 lb (52 390 kg)
Max level speed at 23 500 ft (7 165 m): 509 knots (586 mph; 943 km/h)
Econ cruising speed at 35 000 ft (10 670 m): Mach 0.7
Max rate of climb at S/L, at 100 000 lb (45 355 kg) AUW: 3 760 ft (1 146 m)/min
Operational range: 2 600 nm (2 995 miles; 4 820 km)
Accommodation: Cabin accommodation for three instructors, 12 trainees and four advanced trainees
Equipment: Undergraduate Navigator Training System using Honeywell T-45 electronic simulators. Other equipment includes celestial, radar and inertial navigation systems, LORAN and other radio systems
Ordered by: USA (19 Model 737-253/T-43A)

Photo: T-43A

Long-range troop and freight transport

BRISTOL 175 BRITANNIA (UK)
First flight 1952

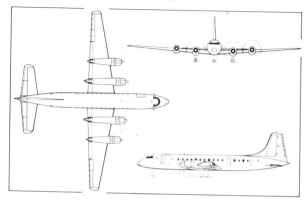

Photo and drawing: Britannia C Mk 1

Data: Britannia C.Mk 1
Power plant: Four Bristol Siddeley Proteus 255 turboprop engines (each 4 310 ehp)
Wing span: 142 ft 3½ in (43.38 m)
Length overall: 124 ft 3 in (37.89 m)
Cabin (Britannia 310):
  Max length 77 ft 5 in (23.60 m)
  Max width 11 ft 7 in (3.53 m)
  Max height 6 ft 8 in (2.03 m)
  Volume (usable) 5 850 cu ft (165.65 m³)
Freight holds (Britannia 310):
  underfloor (two, total) 835 cu ft (23.64 m³)
  above floor 65 cu ft (1.84 m³)
Max payload: 37 400 lb (16 965 kg)
Max T-O weight: 185 000 lb (83 915 kg)
Cruising speed: 310 knots (357 mph; 575 km/h)
Range with max payload: 3 743 nm (4 310 miles; 6 936 km)
Accommodation: Flight crew of 4-6 and up to 139 troops. As an ambulance can accommodate 53 stretchers plus six medical attendants. Quickly-removable seats for freight carrying
Ordered by: Royal Air Force (20 Model 253/C. Mk 1 and 3 Model 252/C. Mk 2)

STOL utility transport, patrol and rescue aircraft

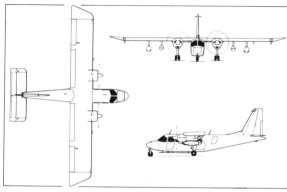

Photo and drawing: Islander
Data: Defender
Power plant: Two Lycoming O-540-E4C5 (each 260 hp) or IO-540-K1B5 six-cylinder piston engines (each 300 hp)
Wing span:
    standard 49 ft 0 in (14.94 m)
    with extended tips 53 ft 0 in (16.15 m)
Length overall: 35 ft 7¾ in (10.86 m)
Passenger cabin, aft of pilot's seat:
    Length 10 ft 0 in (3.05 m)
    Max width 3 ft 7 in (1.09 m)
    Max height 4 ft 2 in (1.27 m)
    Volume 130 cu ft (3.68 m³)

BRITTEN-NORMAN ISLANDER/ DEFENDER (UK)
First flights 1965/1971

Freight capacity incl baggage space: 166 cu ft (4.70 m³)
Baggage space aft of passenger cabin:
    standard 30 cu ft (0.85 m³)
    max 49 cu ft (1.39 m³)
Max T-O weight: 6 950 lb (3 152 kg)
Max level speed at S/L (300 hp engines at 6 600 lb; 2 993 kg AUW): 156 knots (180 mph; 290 km/h)
Cruising speed (75% power) at 7 000 ft (2 135 m), as above: 147 knots (170 mph; 273 km/h)
Max rate of climb at S/L, as above: 1 280 ft (390 m)/min
Absolute ceiling, as above: 17 500 ft (5 340 m)
Max range: over 1 200 nm (1 380 miles; 2 225 km)
Accommodation: Up to 10 persons, including pilot. Can be operated as a freighter, carrying more than a ton of cargo; in this configuration the passenger seats can be stored in rear baggage bay. Ambulance version can carry up to three stretchers and two attendants. Parachutist transport version available
Armament: Optional equipment includes four NATO standard underwing pylons for a variety of external stores, the inboard pair each carrying up to 700 lb (317.5 kg) and the outboard pair up to 450 lb (204 kg) each. Two pairs of 7.62 mm machine-guns and 68 mm SNEB rocket installations are available
Ordered by: Total civil/military orders 446 by mid-1973, including military Islanders for Abu Dhabi (Defence Force 4), Guyana (Defence Force 2), Hong Kong (Air Force 1), Iraq (Air Force 3) and Mexico (Air Force 3).

Passenger (T.7A) and freight (T.7B) transport

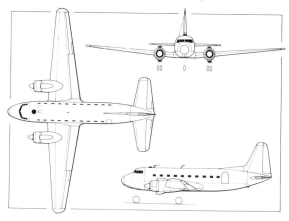

CASA-207 AZOR (Spain)
First flight 1955

Power plant: Two Bristol Hercules 730 fourteen-cylinder radial piston engines (each 2 040 hp)

Wing span: 91 ft 2½ in (27.80 m)

Length overall: 68 ft 5 in (20.85 m)

Max payload:
T.7A 6 806 lb (3 087 kg)
T.7B 8 818 lb (4 000 kg)

Max T-O weight: 36 376 lb (16 500 kg)

Max cruising speed at 12 340 ft (3 760 m): 216 knots (249 mph; 400 km/h)

Max rate of climb at S/L: 1 080 ft (330 m)/min

Service ceiling: 26 250 ft (8 000 m)

Range with crew of 4, 30 passengers and 33 lb (15 kg) of baggage per passenger: 1 408 nm (1 622 miles; 2 610 km)

Range with 6 600 lb (3 000 kg) payload: 1 267 nm (1 460 miles; 2 350 km)

Accommodation: Flight crew of four and 30-40 passengers (T.7A). Alternatively, can be equipped for cargo carrying (T.7B), with large loading door at rear. Other layouts available for paratroop transport, air-dropping of supplies and ambulance duties

Ordered by: Spanish Air Force (10 T.7A and 10 T.7B)

STOL utility transport (T.12), photographic survey aircraft and navigation trainer

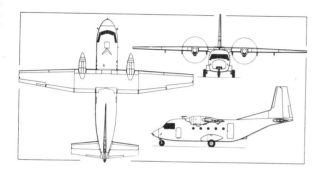

Data: Initial production version
Power plant: Two AiResearch TPE 331-5-251C turboprop engines (each 755 ehp)
Wing span: 62 ft 4 in (19.00 m)
Length overall: 49 ft 10½ in (15.20 m)

CASA C.212 AVIOCAR (Spain)
First flight 1971

Cabin (between flight deck and rear-loading door):
    Length 16 ft 4¾ in (5.00 m)
    Max width 6 ft 10¾ in (2.10 m)
    Max height 5 ft 7 in (1.70 m)
    Volume 618 cu ft (17.50 m³)
Max payload: 4 410 lb (2 000 kg)
Max T-O weight: 13 889 lb (6 300 kg)
Max level speed at 12 000 ft (3 660 m): 194 knots (224 mph; 360 km/h)
Max rate of climb at S/L: 1 713 ft (522 m)/min
Service ceiling: 30 000 ft (9 145 m)
Range at 12 000 ft (3 660 m) with max fuel and 2 303 lb (1 045 kg) payload: 949 nm (1 093 miles; 1 760 km)
Range at 12 000 ft (3 660 m) with max payload: 258 nm (298 miles; 480 km)
Accommodation: Flight crew of two and up to 15 paratroops and an instructor/jumpmaster. Ambulance version normally accommodates 10 stretcher patients and 3 sitting casualties, plus medical attendants, but a change of layout provides for up to 18 stretchers. As a freighter, can carry up to 4 410 lb (2 000 kg) of cargo in the main cabin, including light vehicles. Photographic version equipped with two cameras and a darkroom. Aircrew training version has individual desks for an instructor and five pupils, in two rows, with appropriate instrument installations
Ordered by: Spain (Air Ministry 8 pre-production C.212; Air Force 32 T.12)

Liaison and observation aircraft

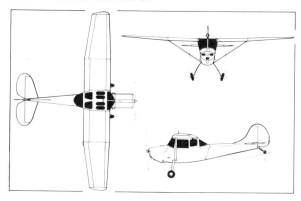

Photo: O-1F with underwing rocket tubes and stores attachments
Drawing: O-1E

CESSNA O-1 BIRD DOG (USA)
First flight 1950

Data: O-1E
Power plant: One Continental O-470-11 six-cylinder piston engine (213 hp)
Wing span: 36 ft 0 in (10.97 m)
Length overall: 25 ft 10 in (7.89 m)
Max T-O weight (alternative mission): 2 430 lb (1 103 kg)
Max level speed: 100 knots (115 mph; 184 km/h)
Max rate of climb at S/L: 1 150 ft (350 m)/min
Service ceiling: 18 500 ft (5 640 m)
Absolute ceiling: 24 800 ft (7 565 m)
Cruising range: 460 nm (530 miles; 848 km)
Accommodation: Pilot and observer in tandem
Ordered by: Air forces of Austria (19 O-1E), Brazil (20 O-1A/E), Canada (22 O-1E), Chile (Army 4 O-1A), France (Army 90 O-1E), Italy (100 O-1E), Japan (Army 100 O-1A and Fuji-built O-1E), Khmer (10 O-1E), South Korea (O-1E), Laos (20 O-1E), Norway (26 O-1E), Pakistan (Army approx 60, plus own production from 1972), Spain (Air Force/Army 8 or more O-1E), Thailand (O-1E), USA (Army approx 2 485 O-1A/G, 310 TO-1D/O-1D/O-1F and approx 550 O-1E; Marine Corps 60 O-1B and 25 O-1C) and South Vietnam (approx 60 O-1A/E)

Forward air control and light strike (0-2A) and psychological warfare aircraft (0-2B)

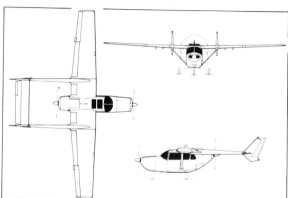

Photo: 0-2A
Drawing: 0-2B
Data: 0-2A
Power plant: Two Continental IO-360-C six-cylinder piston engines (each 210 hp)
Wing span: 38 ft 2 in (11.63 m)
Length overall: 29 ft 9 in (9.07 m)

CESSNA O-2 (USA)
First flight 1967

Cabin:
Length 9 ft 11 in (3.02 m)
Max width 3 ft 8¼ in (1.12 m)
Max height 4 ft 3¼ in (1.30 m)
Volume 138 cu ft (3.91 m³)
Baggage space: 17 cu ft (0.50 m³)
Max T-O weight: 4 630 lb (2 100 kg)
Max level speed at S/L: 179 knots (206 mph; 332 km/h)
Max cruising speed, 75% power at 5 500 ft (1 675 m): 170 knots (196 mph; 315 km/h)
Max rate of climb at S/L: 1 100 ft (335 m)/min
Service ceiling: 18 000 ft (5 490 m)
Range at max cruising speed, standard fuel, no reserve: 677 nm (780 miles; 1 255 km)
Range at econ cruising speed of 128 knots (147 mph; 237 km/h), long-range fuel, no reserve: 1 120 nm (1 290 miles; 2 076 km)
Accommodation: Seating for pilot and co-pilot with dual controls, and up to four passengers. The passenger seats are removable. Space for 365 lb (165 kg) of baggage in four-seat version
Armament: Four underwing pylons for external stores, including rockets, flares and other light ordnance, such as a 7.62 mm Minigun pack
Ordered by: Air forces of Argentine (border police 2 similar Super Skymaster), Ethiopia (1 Skymaster), Iran (12 0-2A), Ivory Coast (3 Reims 337), Niger (2 Reims FR-337) and USA (510 0-2A/B); prototype STOL version (Reims FTMA Milirole) flown in France in 1970

Basic trainer

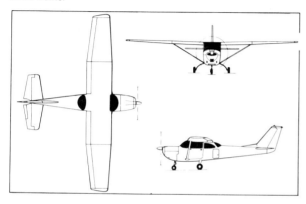

Photo: T-41D
Drawing: T-41A

CESSNA T-41 MESCALERO (USA)
First flight 1964

Data: T-41A
Power plant: One Continental O-300-C six-cylinder piston engine (145 hp)
Wing span: 36 ft 2 in (11.02 m)
Length overall: 26 ft 6 in (8.07 m)
Max T-O weight: 2 300 lb (1 043 kg)
Max level speed at S/L: 120 knots (138 mph; 222 km/h)
Max rate of climb at S/L: 645 ft (197 m)/min
Service ceiling: 13 100 ft (3 995 m)
Range with max fuel at econ cruising speed of 89 knots (102 mph; 164 km/h), no reserve: 625 nm (720 miles; 1 158 km)
Accommodation: Seating for two or four persons, including pilot. Baggage space aft of rear seats, capacity 120 lb (54 kg). Dual controls
Ordered by: Air forces of Colombia (30 T-41D), Ecuador (8 T-41A), Peru (25 T-41A), Saudi Arabia (8 similar Cessna 172), Singapore (8 Cessna 172) and USA (Air Force 204 T-41A and 45 T-41C; Army 255 T-41B)

Utility transport and liaison aircraft

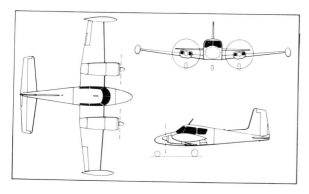

Photo: U-3B
Drawing: U-3A

Data: U-3A

Power plant: Two Continental O-470-M six-cylinder piston engines (each 240 hp)

Wing span: 36 ft 0 in (10.97 m)

Length overall: 27 ft 1 in (8.26 m)

Max T-O weight: 4 700 lb (2 132 kg)

Max level speed at S/L: 201 knots (232 mph; 373 km/h)

Max rate of climb at S/L: 1 660 ft (505 m)/min

Service ceiling: 20 500 ft (6 250 m)

Cruising range (70% power) at 8 000 ft (2 440 m): 738 nm (850 miles; 1 368 km)

Accommodation: Seating for five persons, including pilot. Baggage compartment aft of cabin with capacity of 200 lb (91 kg)

Ordered by: Air forces of France (10 similar Cessna 310), Haiti (1 Cessna 310), Indonesia (1 Cessna 310), Saudi Arabia (1 Cessna 310) and USA (160 U-3A and 35 U-3B)

Short-range troop and cargo transport

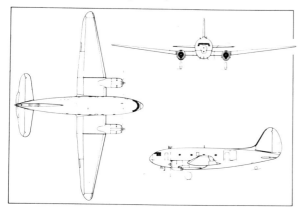

CURTISS-WRIGHT C-46 COMMANDO
(USA)
First flight 1940

Data: C-46A
Power plant: Two Pratt & Whitney R-2800-51 eighteen-cylinder radial piston engines (each 2 000 hp)
Wing span: 108 ft 1 in (32.92 m)
Length overall: 76 ft 4 in (23.27 m)
Cabin (C-46F):
Max length 48 ft 0 in (14.63 m)
Max width 9 ft 10 in (3.00 m)
Max height 6 ft 8 in (2.03 m)
Volume (usable) 2 300 cu ft (65.13 m³)
Underfloor freight holds (total): 455 cu ft (12.88 m³)
Normal max T-O weight: 45 000 lb (20 410 kg)
Max level speed at 15 000 ft (4 570 m): 233 knots (269 mph; 433 km/h)
Max rate of climb at S/L: 1 300 ft (396 m)/min
Service ceiling: 27 600 ft (8 410 m)
Normal range: 1 040 nm (1 200 miles; 1 930 km)
Accommodation: Crew of four and up to 50 troops, 33 stretchers and four attendants, or 16 000 lb (7 257 kg) of freight
Ordered by: Air forces of Dominica (6), Japan (40 C-46D), South Korea (20 C-46D), Peru (3 C-46F), Taiwan (approx 30 C-46D), USA and Zaïre (6)

Basic and advanced trainer and close-support aircraft

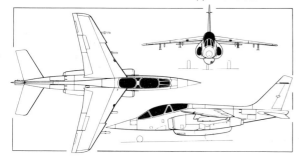

Power plant: Two Turboméca/SNECMA Larzac 04 turbofan engines (each 2 976 lb; 1 350 kg st)
Wing span: 29 ft 11 in (9.12 m)
Length overall (excl nose-probe): 40 ft 3¾ in (12.29 m)
Normal T-O weight (trainer, clean): 9 920 lb (4 500 kg)
Normal T-O weight (weapon training or close support): 13 227 lb (6 000 kg)
Max level speed at high altitude (estimated, at normal T-O weight, clean): Mach 0.85
Max level speed at low altitude (estimated, at normal T-O weight, clean): more than 500 knots (576 mph; 927 km/h)

DASSAULT-BREGUET/DORNIER ALPHA JET
(France/Germany)
First flight 1973

Service ceiling: 49 200 ft (15 000 m)
Ferry range (estimated, at normal T-O weight, clean): 1 078 nm (1 242 miles; 2 000 km)
Accommodation: Crew of two in tandem. Prototypes fitted with Martin-Baker Mk 4 zero-height ejection seats. Cockpits and canopies suitable for installation of Stencel SIIIS or Martin-Baker Mk 10 zero-zero ejection seats
Armament and operational equipment: For armament training and light close-support missions, can be equipped with an underfuselage detachable pod containing a 30 mm DEFA cannon with 150 rds, or a pod with two 0.50 in machine-guns and 250 rds/gun. Provision also for one or two hardpoints under each wing, with non-jettisonable pylons, on which can be carried, within the load capacity of each station, pods of thirty-six 2.75 in rockets; HE or incendiary bombs of 50, 125, 250 or 400 kg; practice launchers for bombs or rockets; or drop-tanks. Provision for carrying a reconnaissance pod. Max permissible load for all five stations is 4 850 lb (2 200 kg). Fire control system for air-to-air or air-to-ground firing, dive bombing and low-level bombing
Ordered by: Belgian Air Force (about 33); air forces of France and German Federal Republic expected to order 200 each, the former for training, the latter for close air support and battlefield reconnaissance

Transport, systems trainer, reconnaissance and communications aircraft

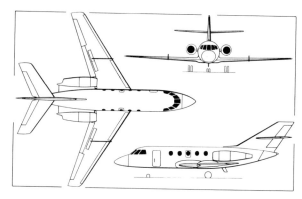

Data: Falcon 20 Series F
Power plant: Two General Electric CF700-2D-2 turbofan engines (each 4 315 lb; 1 960 kg st)
Wing span: 53 ft 6 in (16.30 m)
Length overall: 56 ft 3 in (17.15 m)
Cabin, including fwd baggage space and rear toilet:
Length 23 ft 2¾ in (7.08 m)
Max width 6 ft 1¾ in (1.87 m)
Max height 5 ft 8 in (1.73 m)
Volume 700 cu ft (20.0 m³)

Baggage compartments:
fwd 24.7 cu ft (0.70 m³)
aft 13.1 cu ft (0.37 m³)
Max payload: 3 320 lb (1 500 kg)
Max T-O weight: 28 660 lb (13 000 kg)
Max cruising speed at 25 000 ft (7 620 m) at AUW of 20 000 lb (9 071 kg): 465 knots (536 mph; 862 km/h)
Absolute ceiling: 42 000 ft (12 800 m)
Max range with 8 passengers and 9 240 lb (4 190 kg) fuel, reserves for 150 nm (172 mile; 276 km) flight to alternate plus 45 min, at long-range cruising speed of 381 knots (439 mph; 706 km/h): 1 610 nm (1 850 miles; 2 980 km)
Accommodation: Flight crew of two, with dual controls, and up to 14 passengers. Special equipment installed in Falcon ST enables it to be used for weapon systems training. ECM and radar reconnaissance, and flying command post and communications centre versions available.
Ordered by: Air forces of Australia (3), Belgium (3), Canada (8), Central African Republic (1), France (11, incl two Falcon ST), Ivory Coast (1) and Libya (2 Falcon ST)

Staff transport, communications and training aircraft

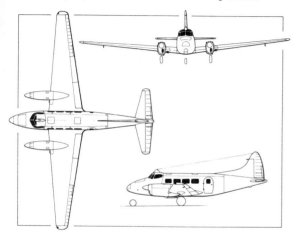

DE HAVILLAND DOVE/DEVON/SEA DEVON (UK)
First flights 1945/1948/1955

Data: Devon C.Mk 2
Power plant: Two Bristol Siddeley Gipsy Queen 175 engines (each 380 hp)
Wing span: 57 ft 0 in (17.40 m)
Length overall: 39 ft 3 in (11.96 m)
Cabin, excl flight deck:
  Length 12 ft 3 in (3.73 m)
  Max width 4 ft 6 in (1.37 m)
  Max height 5 ft 3 in (1.60 m)
  Volume 303 cu ft (8.58 m³)
Freight compartment: 67 cu ft (1.90 m³)
Max payload: 1 477 lb (670 kg)
Max T-O weight: 8 950 lb (4 060 kg)
Max level speed: 200 knots (230 mph; 370 km/h)
Service ceiling: 21 700 ft (6 610 m)
Range with standard fuel and 1 398 lb (634 kg) payload, with allowances for 45 min stand-off and 5% reserves: 764 nm (880 miles; 1 415 km)
Accommodation: Seating for up to 11 persons, including crew
Ordered by: Air forces of Ethiopia (2 Dove Srs 1, 1 Srs 8), India (Air Force 14 Dove; Navy 2 Devon), Irish Republic (1 each Dove Srs 5, 7 and 8), Jordan (2 Dove Srs 8), Lebanon (1 Dove), Malaysia (5 Dove Srs 7/Srs 8/Devon), New Zealand (16 Devon), Paraguay (1 Dove), Sri Lanka (5 Dove), UK (Air Force approx 40 Devon C. Mk 1/2; Navy 13 Sea Devon C. Mk 20) and Zaïre (6 Dove)

Utility transport

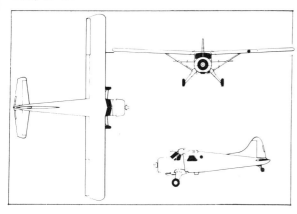

Data: Landplane versions
Power plant: One Pratt & Whitney R-985-AN-1 or AN-3 nine-cylinder radial piston engine (450 hp)

DE HAVILLAND CANADA DHC-2 Mk 1
BEAVER (Canada)
First flight 1947

Wing span: 48 ft 0 in (14.64 m)
Length overall: 30 ft 4 in (9.24 m)
Cabin, incl. cockpit:
  Length 9 ft 0 in (2.74 m)
  Max width 4 ft 0 in (1.22 m)
  Max height 4 ft 3 in (1.30 m)
  Volume 120 cu ft (3.40 m³)
Baggage hold (in rear fuselage): 14 cu ft (0.40 m³)
Max T-O weight: 5 100 lb (2 313 kg)
Max level speed at S/L: 122 knots (140 mph; 225 km/h)
Max rate of climb at S/L: 1 020 ft (311 m) /min
Service ceiling: 18 000 ft (5 490 m)
Range with max fuel, 45 min reserve: 675 nm (778 miles; 1 252 km)
Range with max payload, 45 min reserve: 419 nm (483 miles; 777 km)
Accommodation: Pilot and up to seven passengers or freight. Baggage compartment at rear of cabin
Ordered by: Air forces of Argentine (3), Austria (3), Colombia (10), Dominica (3), Finland (1), Ghana (2), Greece (Army 1), Iran (5), Kenya (10), South Korea, Laos (6 U-6A), Netherlands (9 U-6A), Oman (3), Peru (3), South Yemen (6), Tanzania (3), Thailand (4 U-6A), UK (Army 42 AL. Mk 1), USA (Air Force/Army 968 U-6A, incl some for MAP export), South Vietnam (approx 7 U-6A), Yugoslavia and Zambia (5)

Search and rescue, survey and utility transport aircraft

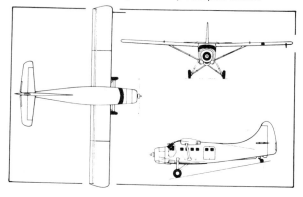

DE HAVILLAND CANADA DHC-3 OTTER
(Canada)
First flight 1951

Data: Landplane version

Power plant: One Pratt & Whitney R-1340 nine-cylinder radial piston engine (600 hp)

Wing span: 58 ft 0 in (17.69 m)

Length overall: 41 ft 10 in (12.80 m)

Cabin, excl flight deck:
Length 16 ft 5 in (5.00 m)
Max width 5 ft 2 in (1.58 m)
Max height 4 ft 11 in (1.50 m)

Max T-O weight: 8 000 lb (3 629 kg)

Max level speed at 5 000 ft (1 525 m): 139 knots (160 mph; 257 km/h)

Max rate of climb at S/L: 850 ft (259 m)/min

Service ceiling: 18 800 ft (5 730.m)

Max range, allowances for 10 min warm-up, T-O, climb to 5 000 ft (1 525 m) and fuel reserves for 45 min at cruise power: 820 nm (945 miles; 1 520 km)

Accommodation: Pilot and co-pilot or passenger side by side on flight deck, and up to 10 passengers in cabin. Passenger seats quickly removable. Alternative accommodation for 6 stretchers and 4 passengers, or 3 stretchers and 7 passengers, or freight

Ordered by: Air forces of Argentine (3), Bangladesh (Defence Force 4), Burma (8), Canada (69), Ghana (12), India (26), Indonesia (7) and USA (Army 6 YU-1, 176 U-1A; Navy 18 U-1B)

STOL tactical transport

DE HAVILLAND CANADA DHC-4 CARIBOU
(Canada)
First flight 1958

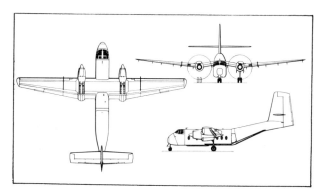

Max payload: 8 740 lb (3 965 kg)
Normal max T-O weight: 28 500 lb (12 928 kg)
Max level speed at 6 500 ft (1 980 m): 188 knots (216 mph; 347 km/h)
Max rate of climb at S/L: 1 355 ft (413 m)/min
Service ceiling: 24 800 ft (7 560 m)
*Range with max fuel: 1 135 nm (1 307 miles; 2 103 km)
*Range with max payload: 210 nm (242 miles; 390 km)
Accommodation: Flight crew of two and up*to 32 troops or 26 fully-equipped paratroops. Up to 22 stretchers, 4 sitting casualties and 4 attendants in ambulance role. Typical freight loads are three tons of cargo or two fully-loaded jeeps
Ordered by: Air forces of Abu Dhabi (5), Australia (31), Cameroun (2), Canada (9 CC-108, of which 4 allocated to UN forces in the Congo), Ghana (8), India (20), Kenya (6), Kuwait (2), Malaysia (16), Muscat & Oman (3), Spain (16), Tanzania (4), Thailand (Police Dept 3), Uganda (Police Air Wing 1), USA (Army 5 YAC-1, and 159 CV-2A/B of which 134 CV-2B transferred to USAF as C-7A), and Zambia (5)

Data: DHC-4A
Power plant: Two Pratt & Whitney R-2000-7M2 fourteen-cylinder radial piston engines (each 1 450 hp)
Wing span: 95 ft 7½ in (29.15 m)
Length overall: 72 ft 7 in (22.13 m)
Cabin, excluding flight deck:
Length 28 ft 9 in (8.76 m)
Max width 7 ft 3 in (2.21 m)
Max height 6 ft 3 in (1.90 m)
Volume 1 150 cu ft (32.57 m³)

* *at long-range cruising speed at 7 500 ft (2 285 m), with allowances for warm-up, taxi, take-off, climb, descent, landing, and 45 min reserve*

83

STOL assault and utility transport

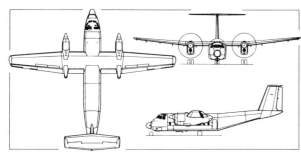

Data: CC-115
Power plant: Two General Electric CT64-820-1 turboprop engines (each 3 055 ehp)
Wing span: 96 ft 0 in (29.26 m)
Length overall: 79 ft 0 in (24.08 m)

DE HAVILLAND CANADA DHC-5 BUFFALO
(Canada)
First flight 1964

Cabin, excluding flight deck:
Length, cargo floor 31 ft 5 in (9.58 m)
Max width 8 ft 9 in (2.67 m)
Max height 6 ft 10 in (2.08 m)
Volume 1 715 cu ft (48.56 m³)
Max payload, STOL transport mission, firm smooth airfield surface: 18 000 lb (8 164 kg)
Max T-O weight, mission and airfield as above: 49 200 lb (22 316 kg)
Max cruising speed at 10 000 ft (3 050 m), mission and airfield as above: 227 knots (261 mph; 420 km/h)
Max rate of climb at S/L, normal rated power, mission and airfield as above: 1 400 ft (427 m)/min
Service ceiling, normal rated power, mission and airfield as above: 24 300 ft (7 405 m)
Range at 10 000 ft (3 050 m) with max payload, mission and airfield as above: 655 nm (754 miles; 1 213 km)
Range at 10 000 ft (3 050 m), zero payload, mission and airfield as above: 1 830 nm (2 107 miles; 3 390 km)
Accommodation: Crew of three and up to 41 troops or 35 paratroops. Up to 24 stretchers and six seats in ambulance role
Ordered by: Air forces of Brazil (24), Canada (15 CC-115), Peru (16) and USA (Army 4 for evaluation, since transferred to USAF as C-8A)

STOL utility transport

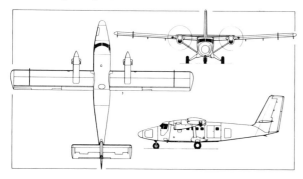

DE HAVILLAND CANADA DHC-6 TWIN OTTER (Canada)
First flight 1965

Cabin, excluding flight deck, galley and baggage compartment:
Length 18 ft 6 in (5.64 m)
Max width 5 ft 3¼ in (1.61 m)
Max height 4 ft 11 in (1.50 m)
Volume 384 cu ft (10.87 m³)
Baggage compartment (nose): 38 cu ft (1.08 m³)
Baggage compartment (rear): 88 cu ft (2.49 m³)
Max payload for 100 nm (115 miles; 185 km): 4 420 lb (2 004 kg)
Max T-O weight: 12 500 lb (5 670 kg)
Max cruising speed at 10 000 ft (3 050 m): 182 knots (210 mph; 338 km/h)
Max rate of climb at S/L: 1 600 ft (488 m)/min
Service ceiling: 26 700 ft (8 140 m)
Range at max cruising speed with 2 550 lb (1 156 kg) payload: 690 nm (794 miles; 1 277 km)
Range at max cruising speed with 2 131 lb (966 kg) payload and wing tanks: 958 nm (1 103 miles; 1 775 km)
Accommodation: One or two pilots and up to 20 passengers. Compartments in nose and aft of main cabin for 300 lb (136 kg) and 500 lb (227 kg) of baggage respectively. Alternative layout for freight carrying
Ordered by: Total orders 380 by mid-1973, including military orders from air forces of Argentine (Air Force 5, Navy 1, Army 3), Canada (8 CC-138), Chile (7), Jamaica (Defence Force 1), Norway (3), Panama (1), Paraguay (1), Peru (11) and Uganda (Police Air Wing 1)

Photo and drawing: Twin Otter Series 300
Data: Series 300
Power plant: Two Pratt & Whitney (UACL) PT6A-27 turboprop engines (each 652 ehp)
Wing span: 65 ft 0 in (19.81 m)
Length overall: 51 ft 9 in (15.77 m)

87

General utility, transport and ambulance aircraft

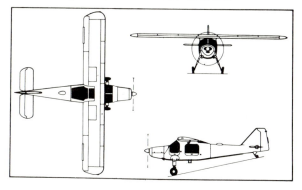

DORNIER Do 27 (Germany)
First flight 1954

Data: Do 27 A-4
Power plant: One Lycoming GO-480-B1A6 six-cylinder piston engine (270 hp)
Wing span: 39 ft 4½ in (12.00 m)
Length overall: 31 ft 6 in (9.60 m)
Cabin, excl flight deck, incl baggage space:
  Length 6 ft 8¾ in (2.05 m)
  Max width 4 ft 3¼ in (1.30 m)
  Max height 4 ft 7 in (1.40 m)
  Volume 95.35 cu ft (2.70 m³)
Baggage space: 8.83 cu ft (0.25 m³)
Max T-O weight: 4 070 lb (1 850 kg)
Max level speed at 3 280 ft (1 000 m): 122 knots (141 mph; 227 km/h)
Max rate of climb at S/L: 650 ft (198 m)/min
Service ceiling: 10 825 ft (3 300 m)
Range at 3 280 ft (1 000 m), 60% power, with max fuel, no allowances: 595 nm (685 miles; 1 100 km)
Accommodation: Seating for up to five persons, or can be used for observation, freight carrying, ambulance or rescue duties. Optional dual controls for training. Provision for carrying and air-dropping supply canisters
Ordered by: Air forces of Belgium (12 Do 27 B), German Federal Republic (Air Force/Army 428), Nigeria (14), Portugal (146 Do 27 A-4), Spain (50 similar CASA C.127), Sweden (Army 5 Do 27 A-4), Switzerland (10 Do 27 H-2), Turkey (Army 15) and Zaïre (2)

Communications, ambulance and utility transport

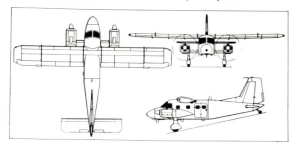

DORNIER Do 28 D SKYSERVANT
(Germany)
First flight 1966

Data: Do 28 D-2 Skyservant
Power plant: Two Lycoming IGSO-540-A1E six-cylinder piston engines (each 380 hp)
Wing span: 51 ft 0¼ in (15.55 m)
Length overall: 37 ft 5¼ in (11.41 m)
Cabin:
Max length 13 ft 0½ in (3.97 m)
Max width 4 ft 6 in (1.37 m)
Max height 4 ft 11⅞ in (1.52 m)
Volume 286 cu ft (8.10 m³)
Max T-O weight: 8 470 lb (3 842 kg)
Max level speed at 10 000 ft (3 050 m): 175 knots (202 mph; 325 km/h)
Cruising speed, 65% power at 10 000 ft (3 050 m): 148 knots (170 mph; 273 km/h)
Max rate of climb at S/L: 1 180 ft (360 m)/min
Service ceiling: 25 200 ft (7 680 m)
Range with max fuel: 1 090 nm (1 255 miles; 2 020 km)
Accommodation: Pilot and either co-pilot or passenger side by side on flight deck. Main cabin accommodates up to 13 persons or five stretchers and five folding seats. Baggage compartments aft of cabin and in nosecone. Alternatively, cabin can be stripped for cargo-carrying
Ordered by: German Federal Republic (Air Force/Army 105, Navy 20) and Turkey (Army 2)

Short-range general-purpose transport

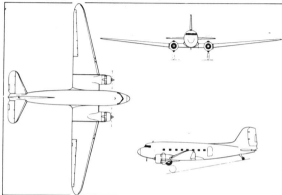

Photo: EC-47 **Drawing and Data:** C-47A
Power plant: Two Pratt & Whitney R-1830-92 fourteen-
cylinder radial piston engines (each 1 200 hp)
Wing span: 95 ft 0 in (28.95 m)
Length overall: 64 ft 5½ in (19.64 m)
Cabin (DC-3C): Max length 30 ft 0 in (9.14 m)
  Max width 7 ft 8 in (2.34 m)
  Max height 6 ft 7 in (2.01 m)
  Volume (usable) 1 245 cu ft (35.25 m³)
Normal max T-O weight: 26 000 lb (11 793 kg)
Max level speed at 8 500 ft (2 590 m): 199 knots (229
mph; 369 km/h)
Service ceiling: 24 100 ft (7 345 m)
Normal range: 1 300 nm (1 500 miles; 2 414 km)

DOUGLAS C-47/C-117 SKYTRAIN (USA)
First flights 1935/1945

Accommodation: Crew of three and 28 troops, or 18
stretchers and attendants, or 6 000 lb (2 722 kg)
freight
Ordered by (C-47 unless stated otherwise): Air forces of
Argentine (Air Force 12; Navy 9; Army 3), Australia,
Belgium (11, incl 3 C-47/NASARR), Bolivia (18), Brazil
(47, incl 2 EC-47), Burma (12), Cameroun (5), Canada
(47 CC-129), Central African Republic (3), Chad (1),
Chile (25), Colombia (8), Congo (2), Dahomey (1 or 2),
Denmark (8), Dominica, Ecuador (C-47/DC-3), El Sal-
vador (5), Ethiopia (4), Finland (8), France (Navy 10),
Gabon (3), German Federal Republic (16, incl 6
C-47/NASARR), Greece (30), Guatemala (8
C-47/DC-3), Haiti (6), Honduras (6), India (90), In-
donesia (Air Force 6; Navy 6), Iran (10), Israel (10),
Italy, Ivory Coast (3), Japan (Navy 4 R4D-6), Jordan
(4), Khmer (11, incl 6 AC-47), South Korea (12
C-47, some AC-47), Libya (9), Malagasy (5), Mali (2),
Mauretania (3), Mexico (6), Morocco (10), Nepal (2),
New Zealand (6), Nicaragua (3), Niger (4), Nigeria (9
DC-3), Norway (4), Panama (4), Paraguay (9), Peru
(19), Philippines (28), Portugal (40), Rhodesia (4),
Senegal (4 C-47/DC-3), Somalia (3), South Africa (48),
South Yemen (4), Spain (50), Sudan (2), Sweden (10),
Syria (6), Taiwan (25), Thailand (25), Togo (1), Turkey
(50), Uganda (6), Upper Volta (2), Uruguay (7), UK
(2), USA (Air Force C-47/AC-47/EC-47/RC-47; Navy
C-47/TC-47 and C-117D; Army C-47), Venezuela (24),
South Vietnam (20 C-47/EC-47, 20 AC-47, 10
RC-47), Yemen, Yugoslavia (6), Zaïre (10) and Zambia
(2) Quantities represent approx numbers in service

93

Long-range transport

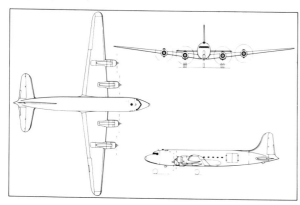

Photo and drawing: C-54D
Data: C-118 Liftmaster
Power plant: Four Pratt & Whitney R-2800-52W eighteen-cylinder radial piston engines (each 2 500 hp)
Wing span: 117 ft 6 in (35.81 m)
Length overall: 105 ft 7 in (32.18 m)
Cabin (DC-6):
    Max length 63 ft 9 in (19.43 m)
    Max width 9 ft 10½ in (3.01 m)
    Max height 7 ft 9 in (2.36 m)
    Volume (usable) 4 107 cu ft (116.30 m³)

DOUGLAS C-54 SKYMASTER/C-118 LIFT-MASTER (USA)
First flights 1942/1946

Freight holds:
    underfloor, total 374 cu ft (10.59 m³)
    above floor, total 144 cu ft (4.08 m³)
Max T-O weight: 107 000 lb (48 535 kg)
Max level speed at 18 100 ft (5 520 m): 312 knots (360 mph; 579 km/h)
Normal range: 3 350 nm (3 860 miles; 6 212 km)
Accommodation: Crew of five and up to 76 passengers or 27 000 lb (12 250 kg) of freight
Ordered by: Air forces of Argentine (Air Force 4 DC-6/C-118; Navy 6 C-54), Belgium (4 DC-6A/C), Bolivia (1 C-54), Brazil (4 C-118/DC-6B), Central African Republic (1 DC-4), Chile (6 DC-6B), Colombia (3 C-54G), Denmark (6 C-54D/G), Ecuador (4 DC-6B), El Salvador (2 C-54), Ethiopia (2 C-54), France (Air Force 1 C-54, 10 DC-6B; Navy 3 DC-4), Gabon (1 DC-6B), German Federal Republic (2 DC-6B), Guatemala (1 C-54), Honduras (1 C-54), Italy (2 DC-6), South Korea (C-54), Mexico (5 C-54, 2 C-118A/DC-6), Niger (2 DC-6B), Nigeria (1 DC-6), Panama (1 DC-6), Paraguay (2 C-54), Peru (4 C-54, 6 DC-6), Portugal (5 C-54/DC-4, 14 HC-54D/E, 11 DC-6A/B), South Africa (5 DC-4), Spain (20 C-54/DC-4), Taiwan (1 DC-6B), Thailand (2 C-54), Turkey (3 C-54), USA (Air Force C-118A; Navy VC-54, C-118B), Venezuela (3 C-54), South Vietnam (1 DC-6B), Yugoslavia (4 DC-6B) and Zaïre (4 C-54). Quantities in most cases represent approx numbers in service, not original orders

Long-range strategic transport

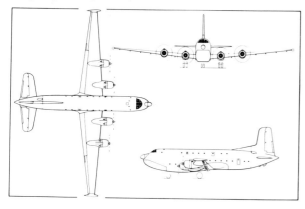

Photo and drawing: C-124C

DOUGLAS C-124 GLOBEMASTER II (USA)
First flight 1949

Data: C-124C
Power plant: Four Pratt & Whitney R-4360-63A twenty-eight-cylinder radial piston engines (each 3 800 hp)
Wing span: 174 ft 2 in (53.08 m)
Length overall: 130 ft 5 in (39.75 m)
Main cargo hold:
Length 77 ft 0 in (23.48 m)
Max width 13 ft 0 in (3.96 m)
Max height 12 ft 10 in (3.91 m)
Volume (usable) more than 10 000 cu ft (283.2 m³)
Max T-O weight: 194 500 lb (88 223 kg)
Max level speed at 20 000 ft (6 100 m): 264 knots (304 mph; 490 km/h)
Range with 26 375 lb (11 963 kg) payload: 3 500 nm (4 030 miles; 6 485 km)
Accommodation: Crew of eight and up to 200 troops, or 127 stretchers plus 52 sitting patients and medical attendants, or up to 68 500 lb (31 070 kg) of freight
Ordered by: US Air Force (204 C-124A and 243 C-124C; most survivors now with Reserve and ANG units)

Long-range strategic transport

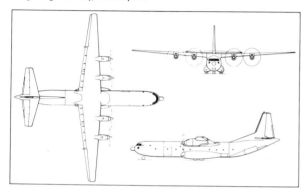

Photo and drawing: C-133B

DOUGLAS C-133 CARGOMASTER (USA)
First flight 1956

Data: C-133B
Power plant: Four Pratt & Whitney T34-P-9WA turboprop engines (each 7 500 ehp)
Wing span: 179 ft 8 in (54.75 m)
Length overall: 157 ft 6 in (48.00 m)
Hold:
Length 90 ft 0 in (27.43 m)
Width 11 ft 10 in (3.63 m)
Usable volume 13 000 cu ft (368 m³)
Normal T-O weight: 286 000 lb (129 730 kg)
Max level speed at 8 500 ft (2 590 m): 312 knots (359 mph; 578 km/h)
Max rate of climb at S/L: 1 315 ft (400 m)/min
Service ceiling: 20 100 ft (6 125 m)
Range with 51 850 lb (23 550 kg) payload: 3 500 nm (4 030 miles; 6 485 km)
Accommodation: Flight crew of four (normal) plus relief crew for extended operation. Accommodation for more than 200 fully-armed troops, or two loadmasters and over 110 000 lb (49 895 kg) of freight
Ordered by: US Air Force (35 C-133A and 15 C-133B)

Short-range general-purpose light transport

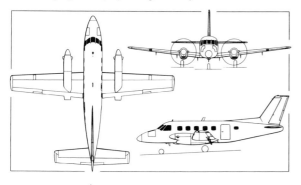

EMBRAER C-95 BANDEIRANTE (Brazil)
First flight 1968

Data: Initial production version
Power plant: Two Pratt & Whitney (UACL) PT6A-27 turboprop engines (each 680 shp)
Wing span: 50 ft 3 in (15.32 m)
Length overall: 46 ft 8¼ in (14.23 m)
Cabin:
  Max length 28 ft 4½ in (8.65 m)
  Width 5 ft 3 in (1.60 m)
  Height 5 ft 3 in (1.60 m)
Max T-O weight: 11 684 lb (5 300 kg)
Max cruising speed at 9 850 ft (3 000 m): 245 knots (282 mph; 454 km/h)
Max rate of climb at S/L: 1 970 ft (600 m)/min
Service ceiling: 27 950 ft (8 520 m)
Max cruising range at 9 850 ft (3 000 m), 30 min reserves: 1 105 nm (1 273 miles; 2 050 km)
Accommodation: Flight crew of two and up to 16 passengers. Conversion into an ambulance for four stretchers takes ten minutes. Baggage compartment at rear of cabin, with total capacity of 46 cu ft (1.30 m³)
Ordered by: Brazilian Air Force (80)

Short/medium-range tactical transport

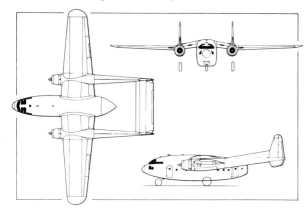

Photo: C-119J
Drawing: C-119G

FAIRCHILD C-119 FLYING BOXCAR (USA)
First flight 1947

Data: C-119K
Power plant: Two Wright R-3350-999 TC18EA2 piston engines (each 3 700 hp) and two General Electric J85-GE-17 auxiliary turbojet engines (each 2 850 lb; 1 293 kg st)
Wing span: 109 ft 3 in (33.30 m)
Length overall: 86 ft 6 in (26.36 m)
Cabin:
Length 36 ft 11 in (11.25 m)
Max width 9 ft 10 in (3.00 m)
Max height 8 ft 0 in (2.44 m)
Volume 3 150 cu ft (89.2 m³)
Max payload: 20 000 lb (9 070 kg)
Max T-O weight: 77 000 lb (34 925 kg)
Max level speed at 10 000 ft (3 050 m): 211 knots (243 mph; 391 km/h)
Ferry range with four 500 US gallon (1 890 litre) Benson tanks: 3 004 nm (3 460 miles; 5 570 km)
Range with max payload: 859 nm (990 miles; 1 595 km)
Accommodation: Flight crew of four, and up to 62 troops or freight
Ordered by: Air forces of Belgium (30 C-119G), India (78 C-119G), Italy (48 C-119G/J), Morocco (6 C-119G), Taiwan (approx 50 C-119G), USA (Air Force 694 C-119F/G, of which 68 cvtd to C-119J, 52 cvtd to AC-119G/K Gunships*, and 8 cvtd to C-119K for Ethiopian Air Force; Navy 58 R4Q-2/C-119F), and South Vietnam (16 C-119G)

* see *Pocket Book of Major Combat Aircraft*

103

Short-range tactical transport

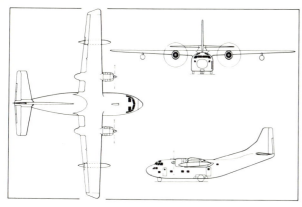

Photo: C-123J
Drawing: C-123B

FAIRCHILD C-123 PROVIDER (USA)
First flight 1949

Data: C-123K
Power plant: Two Pratt & Whitney R-2800-99W radial piston engines (each 2 300 hp) and two General Electric J85-GE-17 auxiliary turbojet engines (each 2 850 lb; 1 293 kg st)
Wing span: 110 ft 0 in (33.53 m)
Length overall: 76 ft 3 in (23.92 m)
Max payload: 15 000 lb (6 800 kg)
Max T-O weight: 60 000 lb (27 215 kg)
Max level speed at 10 000 ft (3 050 m): 198 knots (228 mph; 367 km/h)
Range with max payload: 898 nm (1 035 miles; 1 666 km)
Accommodation: Flight crew of two and 61 troops or 50 stretchers, plus six sitting patients and six attendants, or freight
Ordered by:Air forces of Taiwan (approx 15), Thailand (13), USA (306 C-123B, of which some cvtd to C-123H, 10 to C-123J and 183 to C-123K), Venezuela (18 C-123B) and South Vietnam (approx 50 C-123B)

Instrument, navigation and photographic trainer (IA 35-la), bombing and gunnery trainer/ground attack (-Ib), light transport (-II) and reconnaissance aircraft (-IV)

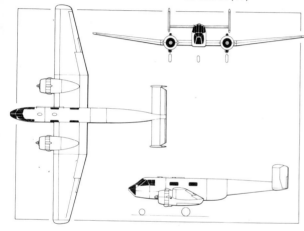

FMA IA 35 HUANQUERO (Argentine Republic)
First flight 1953

Data: IA 35-Ib

Power plant: Two IAR 19A El Indio nine-cylinder radial piston engines (each 650 hp) in early production aircraft; later aircraft have IAR 19C engines (each 840 hp)

Wing span: 64 ft 3¾ in (19.60 m)

Length overall: 45 ft 10½ in (13.98 m)

Max T-O weight: 12 787 lb (5 800 kg)

Max level speed at 6 900 ft (2 100 m): 205 knots (236 mph: 380 km/h)

Max rate of climb at S/L: 1 280 ft (390 m)/min

Service ceiling: 22 975 ft (7 000 m)

Range with standard internal fuel: 674 nm (775 miles; 1 250 km)

Range with max internal fuel (aux tanks): 846 nm (975 miles; 1 570 km)

Accommodation: Flight crew of three (pilot, co-pilot and radio operator), plus instructor and four pupils in -Ia version; two additional crew members in -Ib; or up to seven passengers in -II. Photographer, with Fairchild 225 camera, in -IV

Armament (IA 35-Ib): Two fixed forward-firing 7.65 mm machine-guns. Underwing attachments for four 50 kg or two 100 kg bombs and two 57 mm or eight 127 mm rockets. MK-14 bombsight

Ordered by: Argentine Air Force ordered 100, of which only 47 IA 35-Ia/Ib/II/IV were built; prototype was converted to IA 35-X-III transport. IA 35-III ambulance version projected but not built

Photo and drawing: IA 35-Ia

Short-range light transport, communications, calibration, training and photographic survey aircraft

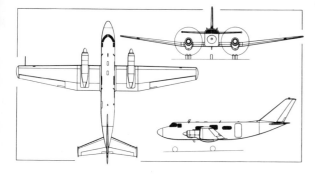

Photo: IA 50 GII with wheel-skis retracted

FMA IA 50 GII (Argentine Republic)
First flight 1963

Power plant: Two Turboméca Bastan VIA turboprop engines (each 930 shp plus 165 lb; 75 kg st)
Wing span (without tip-tanks): 64 ft 3¼ in (19.59 m)
Length overall: 50 ft 2½ in (15.30 m)
Cabin, excl flight deck:
  Max length 16 ft 2 in (4.93 m)
  Max width 4 ft 9 in (1.45 m)
  Max height 5 ft 5½ in (1.66 m)
Max payload: 3 307 lb (1 500 kg)
Max T-O weight:
  with tip-tanks 17 085 lb (7 750 kg)
  without tip-tanks 15 873 lb (7 200 kg)
Max level speed: 269 knots (310 mph; 500 km/h)
Max rate of climb at S/L: 2 640 ft (805 m)/min
Service ceiling: 41 000 ft (12 500 m)
Range with max fuel: 1 389 nm (1 600 miles; 2 575 km)
Range with max payload: 1 076 nm (1 240 miles; 1 995 km)
Accommodation: Crew of two and up to 15 passengers. Utility and paratroop transport version has seven inward-facing seats on port side of cabin and eight on starboard side. Navigation and radar training version has six seats and comprehensive equipment in the cabin. Ambulance version carries two pairs of stretchers on port side and one pair on starboard side, with two seats for attendants. All versions have a forward baggage hold and galley, and a toilet at the rear
Ordered by: Argentine Air Force (37) and Navy (1)

Medium-range troop and freight transport

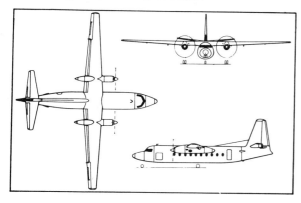

Photo: F.27M Troopship
Data: F.27 Mk 400M Troopship
Power plant: Two Rolls-Royce Dart RDa.7 Mk 532-7R turboprop engines (each 2 210 ehp)
Wing span: 95 ft 2 in (29.00 m)
Length overall: 77 ft 3½ in (23.56 m)
Cabin, excl flight deck:
Length 47 ft 5 in (14.46 m)
Max width 8 ft 4½ in (2.55 m)
Max height 6 ft 7½ in (2.02 m)
Volume 2 136 cu ft (60.50 m³)

Freight holds, max:
fwd 197 cu ft (5.58 m³)
aft 100 cu ft (2.83 m³)
Max T-O weight: 45 000 lb (20 410 kg)
Normal cruising speed at 20 000 ft (6 100 m), at 38 000 lb (17 237 kg) AUW: 262 knots (302 mph; 486 km/h)
Max rate of climb at S/L, AUW of 40 000 lb (18 143 kg): 1 475 ft (450 m)/min
Service ceiling, at 38 000 lb (17 237 kg) AUW: 29 500 ft (9 000 m)
Combat radius: 538 nm (620 miles, 1 000 km)
Max range, no reserves:
standard fuel 1 502 nm (1 730 miles; 2 784 km)
with auxiliary tanks 2 192 nm (2 525 miles; 4 063 km)
Accommodation: Crew of two or three and up to 45 paratroops, 13 283 lb (6 025 kg) of freight or 24 stretchers and 9 attendants or sitting casualties
Ordered by: Air forces of Argentine (12 Mk 400/600 incl 8 Troopships), Ghana (6 Mk 400/600 incl 5 Troopships), Iran (Air Force 20 Mk 400/600 incl 14 Troopships; Navy 4 Mk 400/600 incl 2 Troopships), Ivory Coast (2 Mk 400/600 incl 1 Troopship), Mexico (3 Fairchild FH-227B), Netherlands (3 Mk 100, 9 Mk 300 Troopships), Nigeria (6 Mk 400/600 incl 4 Troopships), Philippines (1 Mk 100), Sudan (4 Mk 400/600 Troopships) and Uruguay (3 Fairchild FH-227B)

Intermediate trainer

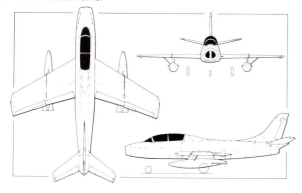

Photo: T1A

Data: T1A

Power plant: One Bristol Siddeley Orpheus 805 turbojet engine (4 000 lb; 1 814 kg st)

Wing span: 34 ft 5 in (10.50 m)

Length overall: 39 ft 9 in (12.12 m)

Max T-O weight (clean): 9 150 lb (4 150 kg)

Max T-O weight with external tanks: 11 000 lb (5 000 kg)

Max level speed at 20 000 ft (6 100 m): 500 knots (575 mph; 925 km/h)

Max rate of climb at S/L (clean): 6 500 ft (1 980 m) /min

Max range with external tanks: 1 050 nm (1 210 miles; 1 950 km)

Accommodation: Crew of two in tandem, on ejection seats

Armament: Provision for one 0.50 in machine-gun in nose, with 220 rounds. Underwing attachments for two 100 Imp gallon (455 litre) drop-tanks, two gun pods, four air-to-surface rockets, two Sidewinder missiles, fourteen 2.75 in air-to-air rockets in M-3 packs, two 750 lb bombs or two napalm bombs

Ordered by: Japan (Air Force 40 T1A and 22 T1B)

STOL utility transport

GAF NOMAD (Australia)
First flight 1971

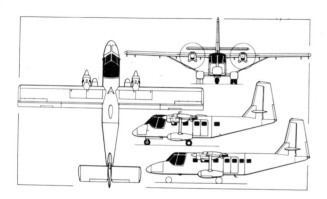

Photo: N22
Drawing: N22 with additional side view of N24

Data: N22
Power plant: Two Allison 250-B17 turboprop engines (each 400 shp)
Wing span: 54 ft 0 in (16.46 m)
Length overall: 41 ft 2⅖ in (12.56 m)

Cabin, excl flight deck and rear baggage compartment:
Length 17 ft 0 in (5.18 m)
Max width 4 ft 3 in (1.30 m)
Max height 5 ft 2⅖ in (1.58 m)
Volume 360.0 cu ft (10.19 m³)
Baggage compartment volume:
nose 28.0 cu ft (0.79 m³)
rear 28.0 cu ft (0.79 m³)
Max payload: 3 200 lb (1 451 kg)
Max T-O weight: 8 000 lb (3 628 kg)
Max cruising speed at S/L: 173 knots (199 mph; 320 km/h)
Max rate of climb at S/L, T-O rating for 5 min: 1 540 ft (469 m)/min
Service ceiling, climbing at 100 ft (30.5 m)/min, max cruise rating: 24 000 ft (7 315 m)
Max range at 90% power, reserves for 45 min hold, at 10 000 ft (3 050 m): 855 nm (985 miles; 1 585 km)
Accommodation: Crew of one or two and up to 12 passengers. Baggage compartments in nose and rear of fuselage
Armament and operational equipment: Provision for four underwing hard-points and two fuselage points each capable of accepting a 500 lb (227 kg) load, including gun and rocket pods. Nose bay can be utilised to accommodate surveillance and night vision aid equipment
Ordered by: Australian Army (9) and Indonesian Air Force (4)

115

COD (Carrier On-board Delivery) transport and instrument trainer

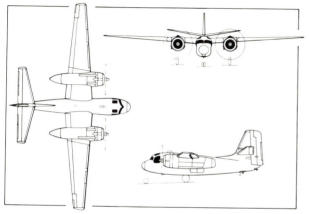

GRUMMAN C-1 TRADER (USA)
First flight 1955

Data: C-1A
Power plant: Two Wright R-1820-82 WA nine-cylinder radial piston engines (each 1 525 hp)
Wing span: 69 ft 8 in (21.23 m)
Length overall: 42 ft 0 in (12.80 m)
Max T-O weight: 24 600 lb (11 158 kg)
Max level speed at 4 000 ft (1 220 m): 244 knots (281 mph; 452 km/h)
Cruising speed: 150 knots (173 mph; 278 km/h)
Max rate of climb at S/L: 1 950 ft (594 m)/min
Range: 837 nm (964 miles; 1 551 km)
Accommodation: Crew of two; folding seats for up to nine passengers, or 3 500 lb (1 587 kg) of freight
Ordered by: US Navy (87, of which 4 converted to EC-1A)

Naval COD (Carrier On-board Delivery) transport

GRUMMAN C-2A GREYHOUND (USA)
First flight 1964

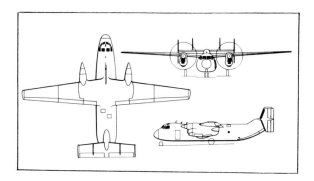

Power plant: Two Allison T56-A-8A turboprop engines (each 4 050 ehp)
Wing span: 80 ft 7 in (24.56 m)
Length overall: 56 ft 8 in (17.27 m)
Cargo space:
Length 27 ft 6 in (8.38 m)
Width 7 ft 3½ in (2.23 m)
Height 5 ft 6 in (1.68 m)
Max payload: 10 000 lb (4 535 kg)
Max T-O weight: 54 830 lb (24 870 kg)
Max level speed at optimum altitude: 306 knots (352 mph; 567 km/h)
Max rate of climb at S/L: 2 330 ft (710 m)/min
Service ceiling: 28 800 ft (8 780 m)
Combat range at average cruising speed of 258 knots (297 mph; 478 km/h) at 27 300 ft (8 320 m): 1 432 nm (1 650 miles; 2 660 km)
Accommodation: Flight crew of two and up to 39 troops, 20 stretchers and four attendants, or freight. Compartment can be adapted to accept Military Airlift Command 463L material handling and support system, with choice of either three 108 x 88 in (2.74 x 2.24 m) master pallets or five 88 x 54 in (2.24 x 1.37 m) modular pallets
Ordered by: US Navy (25)

Search and rescue, transport and general-purpose
amphibian

GRUMMAN HU-16 ALBATROSS (USA)
First flight 1947

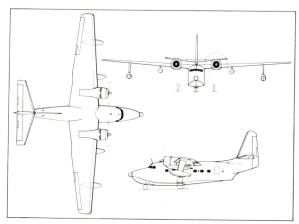

Photo: CSR-110 (HU-16B)
Drawing: HC-16B
Data: HU-16B (ASW version)
Power plant: Two Wright R-1820-76A or -76B nine-
cylinder radial piston engines (each 1 425 hp)
Wing span: 96 ft 8 in (29.46 m)
Length overall: 63 ft 7 in (19.38 m)

Cabin:
Length 26 ft 1 in (7.95 m)
Max width 7 ft 5 in (2.26 m)
Max height 6 ft 4 in (1.93 m)
Volume 568 cu ft (16.08 m³)
Max T-O weight: 35 500 lb (16 100 kg)
Max level speed: 185 knots (213 mph; 343 km/h)
Max rate of climb at S/L: 1 450 ft (442 m)/min
Service ceiling: 22 000 ft (6 705 m)
**Range with max internal fuel, 5% reserve, 30 min
hold:** 2 475 nm (2 850 miles; 4 587 km)
**Max range with two 250 Imp gallon (1 136 litre)
drop-tanks:** 2 849 nm (3 281 miles; 5 280 km)
Accommodation: Standard HU-16B carries crew of three
(five in SAR version) and up to 22 passengers or 12
stretchers. With seats removed, cargo or special equipment can be accommodated. Some aircraft equipped for
anti-submarine duties

Ordered by: Air forces of Argentine (Air Force and Navy,
each 3 HU-16B), Brazil (14 HU-16A), Chile (6
HU-16A), German Federal Republic (Navy 5 HU-16C),
Indonesia (Air Force 8 HU-16A; Navy 5 HU-16A), Italy
(13 HU-16A), Japan (Navy 5 UF-2/HU-16E), Norway
(approx 10 HU-16B), Pakistan (5 HU-16A), Peru (4
HU-16B), Philippines (4 HU-16A), Spain (21
HU-16A/B), Taiwan (HU-16A), Thailand (HU-16A),
USA (Air Force 296 HU-16A/B; Navy 135
HU/LU/TU-16C, of which 51 cvtd to HU-16D; Coast
Guard 34 UF-1G/UF-2G and 37 ex-USAF, all to
HU-16E) and Venezuela (5 HU-16A)

Combat and operational trainer

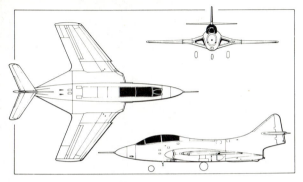

GRUMMAN TF-9J COUGAR (USA)
First flight 1956

Power plant: One Pratt & Whitney J48-P-8A turbojet engine (8 500 lb; 3 855 kg st)
Wing span: 78 ft 4 in (23.88 m)
Length overall, incl nose-probe: 48 ft 6 in (14.78 m)
Normal T-O weight: 20 600 lb (9 344 kg)
Max level speed at S/L: 612 knots (705 mph; 1 135 km/h)
Service ceiling: 50 000 ft (15 240 m)
Range: 868 nm (1 000 miles; 1 610 km)
Accommodation: Pupil and instructor in tandem on Martin-Baker ejection seats
Armament: Provision for two nose-mounted 20 mm cannon and underwing racks for two 1 000 lb bombs, or six HVAR rockets, or four Sidewinder air-to-air missiles and two drop-tanks
Ordered by: Argentine Navy (2) and US Navy (399)

VIP transport (VC-4A) and specialised aircrew trainer (TC-4C)

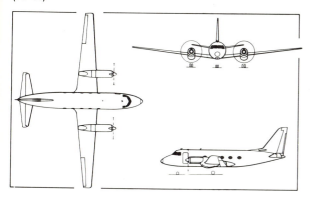

Photo: TC-4C
Drawing: VC-4A

GRUMMAN VC-4/TC-4 GULFSTREAM I
(USA)
First flight 1967 (TC-4C)

Data: TC-4C
Power plant: Two Rolls-Royce Dart Mk 529-8X turboprop engines (each 2 185 ehp)
Wing span: 78 ft 4 in (23.88 m)
Length overall: 67 ft 11 in (20.70 m)
Cabin, excl flight deck:
  Length 33 ft 0 in (10.06 m)
  Max width 7 ft 4 in (2.23 m)
  Max height 6 ft 1 in (1.85 m)
  Volume 1 040 cu ft (29.45 m³)
Max T-O weight: 36 000 lb (16 330 kg)
Max cruising speed: 290 knots (334 mph; 538 km/h)
Max rate of climb at S/L: 1 900 ft (580 m)/min
Service ceiling: 30 400 ft (9 265 m)
Max range: 2 205 nm (2 540 miles; 4 088 km)
Accommodation: Flight crew of two, instructor, and up to six students. Independent and complete A-6A Intruder avionics system in aft cabin, consisting of A-6A training cockpit accommodating a student pilot and student bombardier/navigator, an adjacent instructor's seat, and four student radar/computer readout training consoles linked to the displays in the A-6A cockpit
Ordered by: US Coast Guard (2 VC-4A) and US Navy (9 TC-4C)

Communications transport (HS 125) and navigation trainer (Dominie)

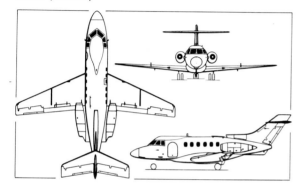

Photo and drawing: Dominie T Mk 1

HAWKER SIDDELEY 125/DOMINIE
T.Mk 1 (UK)
First flight 1962

Data: Dominie T.Mk 1 (HS 125 Srs 2)

Power plant: Two Bristol Siddeley Viper 520 turbojet engines (each 3 000 lb; 1 360 kg st)

Wing span: 47 ft 0 in (14.33 m)

Length overall: 47 ft 5 in (14.45 m)

Cabin:
Length 19 ft 4 in (5.90 m)
Max width 5 ft 11 in (1.80 m)
Max height 5 ft 9 in (1.75m)

Max T-O weight: 21 200 lb (9 615 kg)

Max cruising speed at 25 000 ft (7 620 m): 410 knots (472 mph; 760 km/h)

Service ceiling: 40 000 ft (12 200 m)

Range at max cruising speed: 805 nm (927 miles; 1 492 km)

Range at 365 knots (420 mph; 676 km/h): 1 162 nm (1 338 miles; 2 153 km)

Accommodation: Normal accommodation in Dominie for one pilot, a supernumerary crew member (pilot assister), two students and an instructor. Standard HS 125 accommodation is for flight crew of two and up to 12 passengers in Srs 400 and earlier; crew of two or three and up to 14 passengers in Srs 600

Ordered by: Air forces of Argentine (Navy 1), Brazil (10), Ghana (1), Malaysia (2), Mexico (1), South Africa (7, known as Mercurius) and UK (20 Srs 2/Dominie T. Mk 1, 4 Srs 400/CC. Mk 1 and 2 Srs 600/CC. Mk 2)

Short / medium-range transport

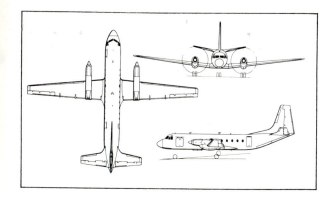

Photo and drawing: Andover C Mk 1·
Data: Andover C. Mk 1
Power plant: Two Rolls-Royce Dart RDa.12 Mk 301 turboprop engines (each 3 245 ehp)
Wing span: 98 ft 3 in (29.95 m)
Length overall: 78 ft 0 in (23.77 m)
Cabin, excl flight deck, incl ramp:
   Length 53 ft 9½ in (16.40 m)
   Max width 8 ft 1 in (2.47 m)
   Max height 6 ft 3 in (1.91 m)
   Volume (usable) 2 200 cu ft (62.3 m³)

HAWKER SIDDELEY 748/ANDOVER 1 & 2
(UK)
First flights 1960/1963

Max payload: 15 350 lb (6 963 kg)
Max T-O weight: 50 000 lb (22 680 kg)
Max cruising speed at 15 000 ft (4 570 m) at AUW of 40 000 lb (18 145 kg): 230 knots (265 mph; 426 km/h)
Max rate of climb at S/L at max AUW: 1 180 ft (360 m)/min
Service ceiling at AUW of 45 000 lb (20 410 kg): 24 000 ft (7 300 m)
Range with max fuel, 8 530 lb (3 870 kg) payload, reserves for 200 nm (230 mile; 370 km) diversion, 30 min hold and 5% block fuel: 1 005 nm (1 158 miles; 1 865 km)
Range with max payload, reserves as above: 245 nm (282 miles; 454 km)
Accommodation: Flight crew of two or three and up to 58 troops, 40 paratroops, 24 stretchers and attendants, or 15 350 lb (6 963 kg) of freight or vehicles. Typical military loads for air-dropping include a Ferret Mk 2/3 scout car and a ¼ ton Land-Rover, or three Land-Rovers
Ordered by: Air forces of Argentine (1 748 Srs 2/2A), Australia (Air Force 10 Srs 2/2A; Navy 2 Srs 2/2A), Brazil (6 Srs 2/2A), Brunei (1 Srs 2/2A), Colombia (SATENA 4 Srs 2/2A), Ecuador (3 Srs 2/2A), German Federal Republic (7 Srs 2/2A), India (4 Srs 1, 41 Srs 2/2A, 48 HAL military freighter version), Tanzania (1 Srs 2/2A), Thailand (2 Srs 2/2A), UK (31 Andover C. Mk 1, 6 Andover CC. Mk 2), Venezuela (1 Srs 2/2A) and Zambia (2 Srs 2/2A)

Basic and advanced trainer, with close-support capability

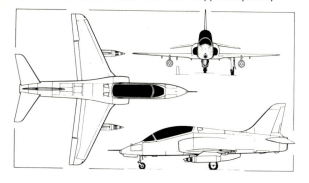

HAWKER SIDDELEY HAWK (UK)
First flight due 1974

Power plant: One Rolls-Royce/Turboméca RT.172-06-11 Adour 151 non-afterburning turbofan engine (5 340 lb; 2 422 kg st)

Wing span: 30 ft 10 in (9.40 m)

Length overall (incl nose-probe): 39 ft 2½ in (11.95 m)

Max T-O weight: approx 15 610 lb (7 080 kg)

Design max speed at 36 000 ft (11 000 m), estimated: 516 knots (595 mph; 1 102 km/h)

Ferry range: approx 1 500 nm (1 725 miles; 2 780 km)

Accommodation: Crew of two in tandem on Martin-Baker Mk 10B rocket-assisted ejection seats. Dual controls standard

Armament and operational equipment: Ferranti F.195 weapon sight and camera recorder in each cockpit. Trainer version has underfuselage centreline attachment for a 30 mm Aden gun and ammunition pack, similar to that in use on the Harrier, and two inboard underwing points each capable of carrying a 1 000 lb (454 kg) stores load. Typical loads include two Matra 155 launchers, each with eighteen 2.75 in air-to-surface rockets, or two clusters of four practice bombs. Provision for two outboard underwing pylons, and a pylon in place of the ventral gun pack, each capable of a 1 000 lb load (i.e. 5 000 lb, 2 270 kg total external stores load), for close-support role. In RAF training roles the normal max external load will probably be about 1 500 lb (680 kg)

Ordered by: Royal Air Force (176 T. Mk 1)

STOL light tactical support aircraft

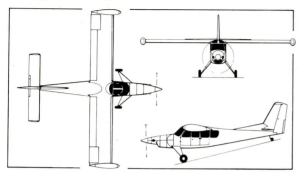

Photo: AU-24A
Drawing: basic Stallion

HELIO AU-24A STALLION (USA)
First flight 1964

Power plant: One Pratt & Whitney (UACL) PT6A-27 turboprop engine (680 shp)
Wing span: 41 ft 0 in (12.50 m)
Length overall: 39 ft 7 in (12.07 m)
Cabin:
  Length 13 ft 6 in (4.11 m)
  Max width 4 ft 2½ in (1.28 m)
  Max height 5 ft 1¼ in (1.56 m)
  Volume 181.4 cu ft (5.14 m³)
Max T-O weight: 6 300 lb (2 857 kg)
Max level speed at 10 000 ft (3 050 m), at 5 100 lb (2 313 kg) AUW: 188 knots (216 mph; 348 km/h)
Range with max fuel, allowances for warm-up, taxying, T-O and climb to 10 000 ft (3 050 m), AUW as above: 557 nm (641 miles; 1 031 km)
Accommodation: Crew of two or three and optionally up to seven extra seats
Armament: Two hardpoints under each wing and a fuselage centreline hardpoint for the mounting of MA4A bomb racks. Each outboard wing station has a capacity of 350 lb (158 kg), each inboard station 500 lb (227 kg), and the fuselage station 600 lb (272 kg). Equipment includes an armament control panel, gunsight, a cabin mounting for a side-firing gun as large as the XM-197 20 mm cannon, and ammunition magazines. Numerous combinations of rockets, bombs and flares can be carried on the five external stores stations
Ordered by: US Air Force (15, of which 14 supplied to Khmer Air Force)

STOL utility and light counter-insurgency aircraft

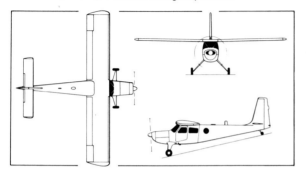

HELIO U-10 SUPER COURIER (USA)
First flight 1958

Data: U-10B Super Courier
Power plant: One Lycoming GO-480-G1D6 six-cylinder piston engine (295 hp)
Wing span: 39 ft 0 in (11.89 m)
Length overall: 31 ft 0 in (9.45 m)
Cabin:
  Length 10 ft 0 in (3.05 m)
  Max width 3 ft 9 in (1.14 m)
  Max height 4 ft 0 in (1.22 m)
  Volume 140 cu ft (3.96 m³)
Baggage space: 15 cu ft (0.42 m³)
Max T-O weight: 3 400 lb (1 542 kg)
Max level speed at S/L: 145 knots (167 mph; 269 km/h)
Max rate of climb at S/L: 1 150 ft (350 m)/min
Service ceiling: 20 500 ft (6 250 m)
Range with standard tanks: 1 198 nm (1 380 miles; 2 220 km)
Accommodation: Pilot and up to five passengers, in three pairs. Second- and third-row seats removable for carrying more than 1 000 lb (454 kg) of freight
Ordered by: Air forces of Peru (5 Courier), Thailand (U-10A) and USA (more than 100 U-10A/B/D)

Air observation post or ambulance

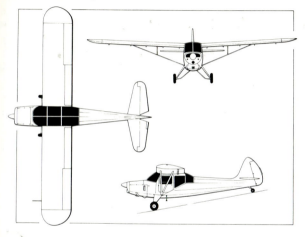

HINDUSTAN HAOP-27 KRISHAK Mk 2
(India)
First flight 1959

Power plant: One Rolls-Royce Continental O-470-J six-cylinder piston engine (225 hp)
Wing span: 37 ft 6 in (11.43 m)
Length overall: 27 ft 7 in (8.41 m)
Design max T-O weight: 2 800 lb (1 270 kg)
Max level speed at S/L: 113 knots (130 mph; 209 km/h)
Max rate of climb at S/L: 900 ft (275 m)/min
Service ceiling: 19 500 ft (5 940 m)
Range with 48 Imp gallons (218 litres) fuel at 6 000 ft (1 800 m) with 6 Imp gallons (27 litres) reserves: 434 nm (500 miles, 805 km)
Accommodation: Crew of two or three. Provision for carrying a stretcher in place of the observer. Dual controls
Ordered by: Indian Army (68)

Basic trainer

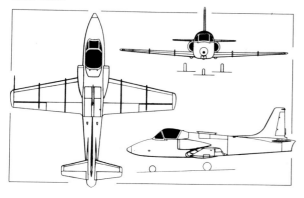

HINDUSTAN HJT-16 Mk I KIRAN (India)
First flight 1964

Power plant: One Rolls-Royce Bristol Viper 11 turbojet engine (2 500 lb; 1 135 kg st)

Wing span: 35 ft 1¼ in (10.70 m)

Length overall: 34 ft 9 in (10.60 m)

Normal T-O weight: 7 936 lb (3 600 kg)

Max T-O weight (with two 50 Imp gallon drop-tanks): 9 039 lb (4 100 kg)

Max level speed at S/L, at normal T-O weight: 375 knots (432 mph; 695 km/h)

Max level speed at 30 000 ft (9 150 m), at normal T-O weight: 371 knots (427 mph; 688 km/h)

Service ceiling, at normal T-O weight: 30 000 ft (9 150 m)

Endurance on internal fuel at 230 knots (265 mph; 426 km/h) at 30 000 ft (9 150 m), at normal T-O weight: 1 hr 45 min

Accommodation: Crew of two side by side on Martin-Baker Mk H4 HA zero-altitude fully-automatic ejection seats

Armament: Provision for conversion to armament training or COIN role, carrying two 7.62 mm twin-gun pods, eight T10 3 in rocket projectiles, twelve 68 mm rockets or four 25 lb practice bombs on underwing pylons

Ordered by: India (Air Force 24 pre-production and 150 production Mk I; latter figure includes some for Navy)

Advanced flying and armament trainer (HA-200) and ground attack aircraft (HA-220)

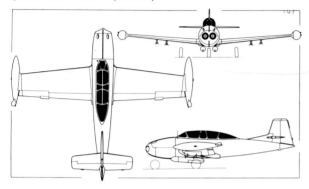

Photo and drawing: HA-220 Super Saeta

HISPANO HA-200 SAETA and HA-220 SUPER SAETA (Spain)
First flights 1955/1970

Data: HA-220 Super Saeta

Power plant: Two Turboméca Marboré VI turbojet engines (each 1 058 lb; 480 kg st)

Wing span over tip-tanks: 35 ft 10 in (10.93 m)

Length overall: 29 ft 5 in (8.97 m)

Max T-O weight with external ordnance: 8 157 lb (3 700 kg)

Max level speed at 23 000 ft (7 000 m), clean: 377 knots (435 mph; 700 km/h)

Max rate of climb at S/L at AUW of 5 840 lb (2 650 kg): 3 346 ft (1 020 m)/min

Service ceiling: 42 650 ft (13 000 m)

Range with max fuel at 29 500 ft (9 000 m), clean: 917 nm (1 055 miles; 1 700 km)

Accommodation: Pilot only (HA-220), in armoured cockpit; no ejection seat. Two seats in tandem in HA-200, with dual controls

Armament and operational equipment: Can be equipped with a variety of guns, rockets and bombs on two underfuselage and four underwing attachments; Maurer type P-2 camera for photographing the results of ground attack missions; Maurer type AN-N6 camera gun; VRM Zeus reflector sight

Ordered by: Air forces of Egypt (10 HA-200 B and up to 90 similar Al-Kahira) and Spain (30 HA-200 A, 55 HA-200 D/E.14, and 25 HA-220/C.10)

Armed light observation helicopter

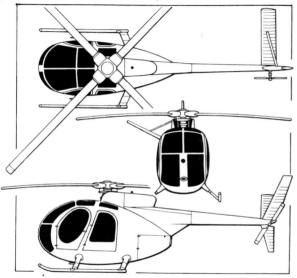

Data: OH-6A
Power plant: One Allison T63-A-5A (250-C18A) turboshaft engine (317 shp, derated to 252.5 shp in OH-6A and 278 shp in Model 500M)
Main rotor diameter: 26 ft 4 in (8.03 m)
Length of fuselage: 23 ft 0 in (7.01 m)

HUGHES OH-6A CAYUSE and MODEL 500M (USA)
First flight 1963

Cabin:
Length 8 ft 0 in (2.44 m)
Max width 4 ft 6 in (1.37 m)
Max height 4 ft 3½ in (1.31 m)
Design gross weight: 2 400 lb (1 090 kg)
Overload gross weight: 2 700 lb (1 225 kg)
Max never-exceed and max cruising speed at S/L, at design gross weight: 130 knots (150 mph; 241 km/h)
Max rate of climb at S/L, at design gross weight: 1 840 ft (560 m)/min
Service ceiling, at design gross weight: 15 800 ft (4 815 m)
Normal range at 5 000 ft (1 525 m), at design gross weight: 330 nm (380 miles; 611 km)
Ferry range (1 300 lb; 590 kg fuel), at design gross weight: 1 354 nm (1 560 miles; 2 510 km)
Accommodation: Crew of two side by side in front of cabin. Two seats in rear cargo compartment can be folded to make room for four fully-equipped soldiers, seated on floor
Armament: Provision for carrying packaged armament on port side of fuselage, comprising XM-27 7.62 mm machine-gun, with 2 000-4 000 rds/min capability, or XM-75 grenade launcher
Ordered by: Air forces of Argentine (Navy 6 Model 500M), Bolivia (12 Model 500M), Colombia (12 Model 500M), Denmark (Army 12 Model 500M), Dominica (7 Model 500M), Japan (Navy 12 Kawasaki OH-6J, Army 125 OH-6J), Mexico (Model 500M), Nicaragua (4 Model 500M), Philippines (6 Model 500M), Spain (Navy 5 Model 500M for ASW duties), Taiwan (6 Model 500 M), and USA (Army 1 434 OH-6A)

143

Light primary training helicopter

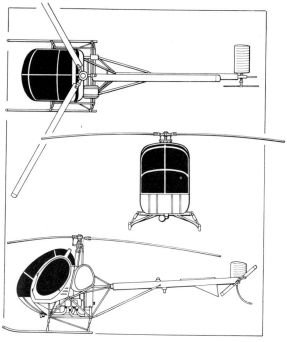

HUGHES TH-55A OSAGE/MODEL 300 (USA)
First flight 1956

Data: TH-55A
Power plant: One Lycoming HIO-360-B1A four-cylinder piston engine (180 hp)
Main rotor diameter: 25 ft 3½ in (7.71 m)
Length of fuselage: 21 ft 11¾ in (6.80 m)
Cabin:
    Length 4 ft 7 in (1.40 m)
    Max width 4 ft 3 in (1.30 m)
    Max height 4 ft 4 in (1.32 m)
Max T-O weight: 1 670 lb (757 kg)
Max level speed at S/L: 75 knots (86 mph; 138 km/h)
Max rate of climb at S/L (mission weight): 1 140 ft (347 m)/min
Service ceiling (mission weight): 11 900 ft (3 625 m)
Range with max fuel, no reserve: 177 nm (204 miles; 328 km)
Accommodation: Two seats side by side. Baggage capacity 100 lb (45 kg)
Ordered by: Air forces of Algeria (7 Model 300), Brazil (Navy 15 Model 300), Colombia (6 Model 300), Ghana (3 Model 300), Kenya (2 Model 300), Nicaragua (2 Model 300) and USA (Army 792 TH-55A)

Light utility transport, communications and photographic aircraft (Pembroke, and Sea Prince C.Mks 1/2), and aircrew trainer (Sea Prince T.Mk 1)

HUNTING PEMBROKE/SEA PRINCE (UK)
First flight 1952/1950

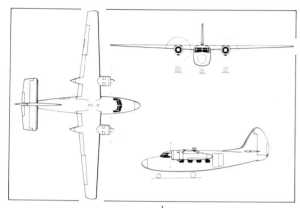

Photo and drawing: Pembroke C Mk 1

Data: Pembroke
Power plant: Two Alvis Leonides Mk 127 nine-cylinder radial piston engines (each 540/560 hp)
Wing span: 64 ft 6 in (19.66 m)
Length overall: 46 ft 0 in (14.02 m)
Max T-O weight: 13 500 lb (6 125 kg)
Max level speed at 2 000 ft (610 m): 195 knots (224 mph; 360 km/h)
Max rate of climb at S/L: 1 070 ft (326 m)/min
Service ceiling: 22 000 ft (6 705 m)
Range: 998 nm (1 150 miles; 1 850 km)
Accommodation: Flight crew of two and up to eight passengers (10 in Mk 52) or freight
Ordered by: Air forces of Belgium (4 Mk 51), German Federal Republic (33 Mk 54), Sudan (3 Mks 54/55), Sweden (10 Mk 52/Tp 83), UK (Air Force 46 Pembroke C. Mk 1 and 6 C(PR). Mk 1; Navy 3 Sea Prince C Mk 1, 4 Sea Prince C. Mk 2 and 8 Sea Prince T. Mk 1), Zaïre (4, probably Mk 51) and Zambia (2 ex-Rhodesian C. Mk 1)

Light transport

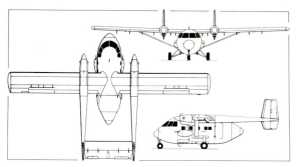

IAI-201 ARAVA (Israel)
First flight 1971

Power plant: Two Pratt & Whitney (UACL) PT6A-34 turboprop engines (each 783 ehp)

Wing span: 69 ft 6 in (20.88 m)

Length overall: 42 ft 7½ in (12.99 m)

Cabin, excluding flight deck and hinged tailcone:
Length 12 ft 8¼ in (3.87 m)
Max width 7 ft 8 in (2.33 m)
Max height 5 ft 8½ in (1.74 m)
Volume 466.2 cu ft (13.2 m³)

Baggage compartment volume: 91.8 cu ft (2.60 m³)

Cargo door volume: 113 cu ft (3.20 m³)

Max payload: 5 570 lb (2 526 kg)

Max T-O weight: 15 000 lb (6 803 kg)

Max level speed at 10 000 ft (3 050 m): 176 knots (203 mph; 326 km/h)

Max rate of climb at S/L: 1 564 ft (477 m)/min

Service ceiling: 26 575 ft (8 100 m)

Range with max fuel, 45 min reserves: 700 nm (806 miles; 1 297 km)

Range with max payload, 45 min reserves: 175 nm (201 miles; 323 km)

Accommodation: Crew of one or two and up to 24 fully-equipped troops or 16 paratroops and two dispatchers. Alternative layouts accommodate 12 stretchers and two sitting patients / medical attendants or freight. Typical freight load is a jeep-mounted recoil-less rifle and its four-man crew

Ordered by: Air forces of Israel (number not known), Mexico (5) and Nicaragua

NATO Code Name *Crate*
Short-range general-purpose transport

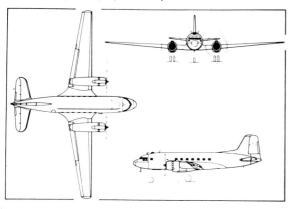

ILYUSHIN Il-14 (USSR)
First flight 1953

Data: Il-14M

Power plant: Two Shvetsov ASh-82T fourteen-cylinder radial piston engines (each 1 900 hp)

Wing span: 103 ft 11 in (31.67 m)

Length overall: 73 ft 3½ in (22.34 m)

Cabin:
Max length 36 ft 0 in (10.97 m)
Max width 9 ft 1 in (2.77 m)
Max height 7 ft 8 in (2.03 m)

Max T-O weight: 38 030 lb (17 250 kg)

Max level speed at 7 875 ft (2 400 m): 224 knots (258 mph; 416 km/h)

Max rate of climb at S/L: 945 ft (288 m)/min

Range: 814 nm (937 miles; 1 508 km)

Accommodation: Flight crew of three and up to 28 passengers

Ordered by: Air forces of Afghanistan (25), Albania (3), Algeria (12), Bulgaria (10), China, Cuba (20), Czechoslovakia (more than 30 similar Avia-14T), Egypt (40), German Democratic Republic (20 Il-14P), Guinea, Hungary, India (22), Indonesia (25), Iraq, Khmer (1), North Korea, Mongolia, Poland, Romania (20), Syria (8), USSR, North Vietnam (12), Yemen and Yugoslavia (13 Il-14S). All quantities estimated

NATO Code Name *Coot*
Troop and personnel transport

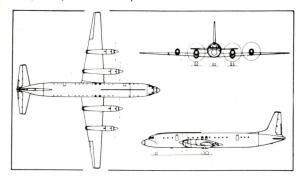

Data: Il-18D

Power plant: Four Ivchenko Al-20M turboprop engines (each 4 250 ehp)

Wing span: 122 ft 8½ in (37.40 m)

Length overall: 117 ft 9 in (35.90 m)

Cabin, excluding flight deck:
Length approx 79 ft 0 in (24.00 m)
Max width 10 ft 7 in (3.23 m)
Max height 6 ft 6¾ in (2.00 m)
Volume 8 405 cu ft (238 m³)

Baggage and freight holds (underfloor and aft of cabin: total): 1 035 cu ft (29.3 m³)

Max payload: 29 750 lb (13 500 kg)

Max T-O weight: 141 100 lb (64 000 kg)

Max cruising speed: 364 knots (419 mph; 675 km/h)

Range with max fuel, 1 hr reserve: 3 508 nm (4 040 miles; 6 500 km)

Range with max payload, 1 hr reserve: 1 997 nm (2 300 miles; 3 700 km)

Accommodation: Flight crew of five and up to 110 passengers (standard) or 122 (max). Cargo holds under floor, forward and aft of wing, and a further hold aft of the rear pressure bulkhead

Ordered by: Air forces of Afghanistan (2 or more), Algeria (4), Bulgaria (5), China, Czechoslovakia, Guinea (2), Poland (2), Romania (1), USSR and Yugoslavia (2); all quantities estimated. Il-38 anti-submarine version described in the *Pocket Book of Major Combat Aircraft*

Crash rescue, firefighting, liaison and utility helicopter

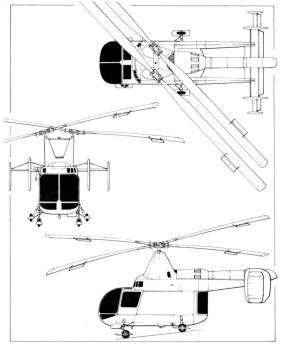

KAMAN H-43 HUSKIE (USA)
First flight 1956

Photo: HH-43F
Data: HH-43F
Power plant: One Lycoming T53-L-11A turboshaft engine
(1 150 ehp, derated to 825 shp)
Diameter of rotors: 47 ft 0 in (14.33 m)
Length of fuselage: 25 ft 2 in (7.67 m)
Cabin:
Max width 5 ft 3 in (1.60 m)
Max height: 3 ft 10 in (1.17 m)
Max payload: 3 970 lb (1 800 kg)
Max T-O weight: 9 150 lb (4 150 kg)
**Max level speed at S/L, at normal T-O weight of 6 500
lb (2 950 kg):** 104 knots (120 mph; 193 km/h)
Max rate of climb at S/L, weight as above: 1 800 ft
(550 m)/min
Service ceiling, weight as above: 23 000 ft (7 010 m)
**Range at 5 000 ft (1 525 m) at T-O weight of 8 270 lb
(3 750 kg), no allowances:** 438 nm (504 miles; 811 km)
Accommodation: Pilot, two fully-clothed firefighters and
1 000 lb (454 kg) of firefighting and rescue gear.
Alternative accommodation for pilot, co-pilot and 10
passengers; or pilot, four stretchers and a medical
attendant
Ordered by: Air forces of Burma (12 HH-43B), Colombia
(6 HH-43B), Iran (17 HH-43F), Morocco (4 HH-43B),
Pakistan (6 HH-43B), Thailand (3 HH-43B) and USA
(Air Force 18 HH-43A, 193 HH-43B and 40 HH-43F)

Medium-range troop and freight transport

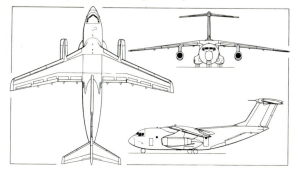

KAWASAKI C-1 (Japan)
First flight 1970

Power plant: Two Pratt & Whitney JT8D-9 turbofan engines (each 14 500 lb; 6 575 kg st)
Wing span: 100 ft 4¾ in (30.60 m)
Length overall: 95 ft 1¾ in (29.00 m)
Cabin:
    Max length 34 ft 9¼ in (10.60 m)
    Max width 11 ft 9¾ in (3.60 m)
    Max height 8 ft 4½ in (2.55 m)
Normal payload: 17 640 lb (8 000 kg)
Max T-O weight: 85 320 lb (38 700 kg)
Max level speed at 25 000 ft (7 620 m) at 78 150 lb (35 450 kg) AUW: 440 knots (507 mph; 815 km/h)
Max rate of climb at S/L at max T-O weight: 3 880 ft (1 173 m)/min
Service ceiling at 78 150 lb (35 450 kg) AUW: 39 375 ft (12 000 m)
Range with max fuel and payload of 5 730 lb (2 600 kg): 1 780 nm (2 050 miles; 3 300 km)
Range with 17 640 lb (8 000 kg) payload: 700 nm (807 miles; 1 300 km)
Accommodation: Crew of five (including load supervisor) and up to 60 troops, 45 paratroops, 36 stretchers and attendants, or freight. As a freight carrier, loads can include a 2½ ton truck, a 105 mm howitzer, two ¾ ton trucks or three jeeps. Up to three pre-loaded freight pallets, 7 ft 4 in (2.24 m) wide and 9 ft 0 in (2.74 m) long, can be carried
Ordered by: Japan (Air Force 2 pre-production and 22 production C-1)

Long-range strategic heavy transport

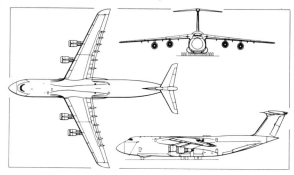

Power plant: Four General Electric TF39-GE-1 turbofan engines (each 41 000 lb; 18 600 kg st)
Wing span: 222 ft 8½ in (67.88 m)
Length overall: 247 ft 10 in (75.54 m)
Cabins, excluding flight deck:
  Length: upper deck, forward 39 ft 4 in (11.99 m)
    upper deck, aft 59 ft 8½ in (18.20 m)
    lower deck, without ramp 121 ft 1 in (36.91 m)
    lower deck, with ramp 144 ft 7 in (44.07 m)
  Max width: upper deck, forward 13 ft 9½ in (4.20 m)
    upper deck, aft 13 ft 0 in (3.96 m)
    lower deck 19 ft 0 in (5.79 m)
  Max height: upper deck 7 ft 6 in (2.29 m)
    lower deck 13 ft 6 in (4.11 m)
  Volume: upper deck, forward 2 010 cu ft (56.91 m³)

upper deck, aft 6 020 cu ft (170.46 m³)
  lower deck 34 795 cu ft (985.29 m³)
Design max payload: 265 000 lb (120 200 kg)
Max T-O weight: 764 500 lb (346 770 kg)
Max level speed at 25 000 ft (7 620 m): 496 knots (571 mph; 919 km/h)
Max rate of climb at S/L, at long-range mission weight of 712 000 lb (322 958 kg), at maximum rated thrust: 2 500 ft (762 m)/min
Service ceiling at AUW of 615 000 lb (278 950 kg): 34 000 ft (10 360 m)
Range with 220 000 lb (99,790 kg) payload at 440 knots (507 mph; 815 km/h)TAS: 3 050 nm (3 512 miles; 5 652 km)
Range with 112 600 lb (51 074 kg) payload at 728 000 lb (330 200 kg) AUW: 5 500 nm (6 333 miles; 10 191 km)

Accommodation: Normal crew of five, incl loadmaster, with rest area for 15 people (relief crew, couriers etc). Basic version has seats for 75 troops on upper deck. Provision for 270 troops on lower deck, but aircraft is intended primarily as freighter. Typical loads include two M-60 tanks or sixteen ¾ ton lorries; or one M-60 and two Bell Iroquois helicopters, five M-113 personnel carriers, one M-59 2½ ton truck and an M-151 ¼ ton truck; or 10 Pershing missiles with tow and launch vehicles; or 36 standard 463L load pallets. Provision for Aerial Delivery System (ADS) kits for paratroops or cargo
Ordered by: US Air Force (81)

Tactical troop, freight and special-purpose transport

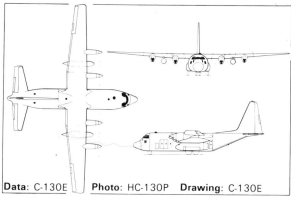

Data: C-130E **Photo:** HC-130P **Drawing:** C-130E

Power plant: Four Allison T56-A-7 turboprop engines (each 4 050 ehp)
Wing span: 132 ft 7 in (40.41 m)
Length overall: 97 ft 9 in (29.78 m)
Cabin, excluding flight deck: Length 41 ft 5 in (12.60 m)
  Length with ramp 51 ft 8½ in (15.73 m)
  Max width 10 ft 3 in (3.13 m)
  Max height 9 ft 2¾ in (2.81 m)
  Volume, including ramp 4 300 cu ft (121.7 m³)
Max payload: 45 000 lb (20 412 kg)
Max normal T-O weight: 155 000 lb (70 310 kg)
Max overload T-O weight: 175 000 lb (79 380 kg)
Max cruising speed: 320 knots (368 mph; 592 km/h)

LOCKHEED C-130 HERCULES (USA)
First flight 1954

Max rate of climb at S/L: 1 830 ft (558 m)/min
Service ceiling at 155 000 lb AUW: 23 000 ft (7 010 m)
Range with max payload, 5% reserve and allowance for 30 min at S/L: 2 100 nm (2 420 miles; 3 895 km)
Range with max fuel, including two 1 360 US gallon external tanks, 20 000 lb (9 070 kg) payload and reserves of 5% initial fuel plus 30 min at S/L: 4 080 nm (4 700 miles; 7 560 km)
Accommodation: Flight crew of four and 92 troops 64 paratroops, or 74 stretchers and 2 attendants. Cargo loads can include a 26 640 lb (12 080 kg) type F.6 refuelling trailer, a 155 mm howitzer and its high speed tractor, or six pre-loaded freight pallets.
Ordered by: Air forces of Argentine (3 C-130E, 3 C-130H), Australia (12 C-130A, 12 C-130E), Belgium (12 C-130H), Brazil (11 C-130E), Canada (24 C-130H), Chile (2 C-130H), Colombia (2 C-130E), Denmark (3 C-130H), Indonesia (8 C-130B), Iran (28 C-130E and 28 C-130H), Israel (20 C-130H), Italy (14 C-130H), Kuwait, Libya (8 C-130E), New Zealand (5 C-130H), Norway (6 C-130H), Pakistan (7 C-130B), Peru (6 L 100-20), Saudi Arabia (10 C-130E, 4 HC-130P), South Africa (7 C-130B), Sweden (2 C-130E), Turkey (7 C-130E), UK (66 C-130K/C. Mk 1/W. Mk 2), USA (Air Force 461 C-130A/B, 389 C/AC/DC/WC-130E, 63 HC-130H/P, 15 HC-130N; Navy 12 C-130E, 7 C-130F, 8 EC-130Q, LC-130R; Marine Corps 46 KC-130F; Coast Guard 1 C-130E, EC-130E, 3 HC-130H), Venezuela (4 C-130H) and Zaïre (3 C-130H)

Communications inspection (C-140A) and special transport (VC-140B)

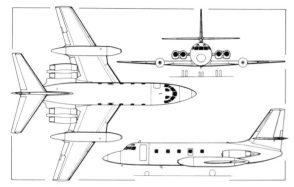

Photo: VC-140B

LOCKHEED C-140 JETSTAR (USA)
First flight 1957

Data: Standard civil JetStar (VC-140B similar)

Power plant: Four Pratt & Whitney JT12A-8 turbojet engines (each 3 300 lb; 1 497 kg st)

Wing span: 54 ft 5 in (16.60 m)

Length overall: 60 ft 5 in (18.42 m)

Cabin, excl flight deck:
Length 28 ft 2½ in (8.59 m)
Max width 6 ft 2½ in (1.89 m)
Max height 6 ft 1 in (1.85 m)
Volume 850 cu ft (24.07 m³)

Max payload: 2 926 lb (1 327 kg)

Max T-O weight: 42 000 lb (19 051 kg)

Max level speed at 23 000 ft (7 010 m): 495 knots (570 mph; 917 km/h)

Max rate of climb at S/L, at AUW of 38 000 lb (17 235 kg): 5 200 ft (1 585 m)/min.

Service ceiling, AUW as above: 37 400 ft (11 400 m)

Range with max payload, step climb, 45 min reserve: 1 840 nm (2 120 miles; 3 410 km)

Accommodation (VC-140B): Flight crew of three and up to 13 passengers

Ordered by: Air forces of German Federal Republic (3), Indonesia (1), Libya (1), Mexico (1), Saudi Arabia (2) and USA (5 C-140A and 11 VC-140B)

Long-range strategic freighter or troop transport

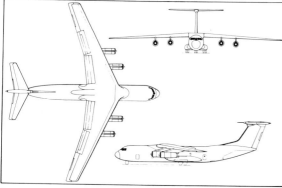

Power plant: Four Pratt & Whitney TF33-P-7 turbofan engines (each 21 000 lb; 9 525 kg st)
Wing span: 159 ft 11 in (48.74 m)
Length overall: 145 ft 0 in (44.20 m)
Cabin, excl flight deck:
 Length, without ramp 70 ft 0 in (21.34 m)
 Length, with ramp 81 ft 0 in (24.69 m)
 Max width 10 ft 3 in (3.12 m)
 Max height 9 ft 1 in (2.77 m)
 Volume, including ramp area 8 730 cu ft (247.2 m³)
Max payload: 70 847 lb (32 136 kg)
Max payload (version able to carry Minuteman ICBM): 86 207 lb (39 103 kg)
Max T-O weight (Minuteman version): 300 600 lb (136 350 kg)

LOCKHEED C-141A STARLIFTER (USA)
First flight 1963

Max level speed at 25 000 ft (7 620 m): 496 knots (571 mph; 919 km/h)
Max level speed at 25 000 ft (7 620 m) (Minuteman version): 485 knots (559 mph; 900 km/h)
Max cruising speed at 24 250 ft (7 400 m): 490 knots (564 mph; 908 km/h)
Max cruising speed at 24 250 ft (7 400 m) (Minuteman version): 478 knots (551 mph; 887 km/h)
Max rate of climb at S/L: 3 100 ft (945 m)/min
Max rate of climb at S/L (Minuteman version): 3 700 ft (1 128 m)/min
Service ceiling at 250 000 lb (113 400 kg) AUW: 41 600 ft (12 680 m)
Range with max fuel and 31 870 lb (14 460 kg) payload, 5% fuel reserve, plus 30 min at S/L: 5 330 nm (6 140 miles; 9,880 km)
Range with design payload, 5% fuel reserve, plus 30 min at S/L: 3 540 nm (4 080 miles; 6 565 km)
Range with design payload, MAC fuel reserve (Minuteman version): 2 180 nm (2 510 miles; 4 040 km)
Accommodation: Flight crew of four. Main cabin accommodates 154 troops or 123 fully-equipped paratroops in fore-and-aft seating, or 80 litters with seats for up to 16 ambulatory patients and/or medical attendants. With "comfort pallet" (toilet and galley) at forward end of cabin, accommodation is reduced to 120 passenger seats. Up to 5 283 cu ft (149.6 m³) of freight can be loaded on ten pallets, using the integral USAF Type 463L loading system
Ordered by: US Air Force (284)

Fighter and light attack aircraft (F-80C and AT-33A) and advanced trainer (T-33A)

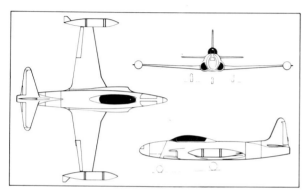

Photo: CL-30 Silver Star (T-33A)
Drawing: T-33A

Data: T-33A
Power plant: One Allison J33-A-35 turbojet engine (5 200 lb; 2 360 kg st)
Wing span: 38 ft 10½ in (11.85 m)
Length overall: 37 ft 9 in (11.51 m)

LOCKHEED F-80C SHOOTING STAR
T-33A (USA)
First flight 1948

Normal T-O weight: 11 965 lb (5 432 kg)
Max level speed at S/L: 521 knots (600 mph; 965 km/h)
Time to 25 000 ft (7 620 m): 6 min 30 sec
Service ceiling: 47 500 ft (14 480 m)
Range: 1 168 nm (1 345 miles; 2 165 km)
Accommodation: Two seats in tandem
Armament: Provision for two 0.50 in machine-guns
Ordered by: Air forces of Belgium (15 T-33A), Brazil (T-33A, 54 AT-33A), Burma (12 AT-33A), Canada (158 T-33A), Chile (10 F-80C, 8 T-33A), Colombia (AT-33A, 10 T-33A), Denmark (18 T-33A), Ecuador (9 F-80C, T-33A), Ethiopia (11 T-33A, 2 RT-33A), France (150 T-33A), German Federal Republic (30 T-33A), Greece (40 T-33A), Guatemala (5 T-33A), Honduras (3 T-33A), Iran (T-33A, 16 RT-33A), Italy (T-33A, RT-33A), Japan (186 T-33A), South Korea (T-33A), Laos (3 T-33A), Libya (3 T-33A), Mexico (15 AT-33A), Netherlands (50 T-33A), Nicaragua (4 T-33B), Pakistan (12 T-33A, 3 RT-33A), Peru (10 AT-33A), Philippines (10 T-33A), Portugal (24 T-33A), Saudi Arabia (13 T-33A), Spain (75 T-33A), Taiwan (T-33A), Thailand (6 T-33A, 2 RT-33A), Turkey (50 T-33A), Uruguay (6 F-80C, 6 AT-33A), USA (Air Force T-33A, AT-33A; Navy T-33B) and Yugoslavia (70 T-33A, 20 RT-33A). Quantities in most cases represent approx numbers in service, not original orders

Light utility transport

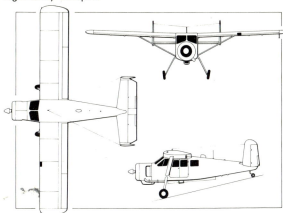

Power plant: One Pratt & Whitney R-985-AN-1 nine-cylinder radial piston engine (450 hp)
Wing span: 45 ft 1¼ in (13.75 m)
Length overall: 28 ft 4½ in (8.65 m)

MAX HOLSTE M.H.1521 BROUSSARD
(France)
First flight 1952

Cabin:
   Length 10 ft 1 in (3.08 m)
   Width 4 ft 1 in (1.52 m)
   Mean height 4 ft 5 in (1.35 m)
   Volume 169.4 cu ft (4.80 m³)
Normal T-O weight: 5 511 lb (2 500 kg)
Max level speed at 3 280 ft (1 000 m), at normal T-O weight: 146 knots (168 mph; 270 km/h)
Max rate of climb at S/L, at normal T-O weight: 1 082 ft (330 m)/min
Service ceiling at normal T-O weight: 18 050 ft (5 500 m)
Range: 647 nm (745 miles; 1 200 km)
Accommodation: Seating for six persons, including pilot. Rear four seats removable for carrying freight or two stretchers and two sitting patients or attendants
Ordered by: Air forces of Argentine (6), Cameroun (7), Central African Republic (7), Chad (3), Congo (3), Dahomey (1 or 2), France (Air Force 190; Navy 40), Gabon (4), Ivory Coast (4), Malagasy (3), Mauritania (6), Morocco (6), Niger (4), Portugal (4), Senegal (5) and Togo (1 or 2)

MBB HFB 320 HANSA (Germany)
First flight 1964

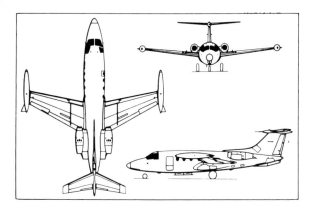

Power plant (36th and subsequent aircraft): Two General Electric CJ610-9 turbojet engines (each 3 100 lb; 1 406 kg st)

Wing span over tip-tanks: 47 ft 6 in (14.49 m)

Length overall: 54 ft 6 in (16.61 m)

Cabin, excluding flight deck, but including toilet etc:
Length 15 ft 0 in (4.58 m)
Max width 6 ft 2¾ in (1.90 m)
Max height 5 ft 9 in (1.75 m)
Volume 435 cu ft (12.32 m³)

Baggage hold (rear) volume: 35 cu ft (1.00 m³)

Max payload (basic):
Passenger version 3 913 lb (1 775 kg)
Freighter version 4 000 lb (1 814 kg)

Max T-O weight (normal): 20 280 lb (9 200 kg)

Max cruising speed at 25 000 ft (7 620 m) at mean weight of 16 530 lb (7 500 kg): 446 knots (513 mph; 825 km/h)

Max rate of climb at S/L, AUW as above: 4 250 ft (1 295 m)/min

Max operating altitude: 40 000 ft (12 200 m)

Range with 6 passengers and baggage (1 200 lb; 545 kg payload), 45 min reserves: 1 278 nm (1 472 miles; 2 370 km)

Accommodation: Flight crew of two and seven to twelve passengers, or freight. Some aircraft equipped for aircrew training, instrument calibration, ECM and other specialised duties

Ordered by: Federal German Air Force (8 VIP transport, 6 ECM and 10 calibration)

Aeromedical transport (C-9A Nightingale) and Fleet support transport (C-9B Skytrain II)

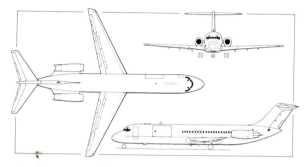

Photo: C-9B Skytrain II
Drawing: C-9A Nightingale

MCDONNELL DOUGLAS C-9 NIGHTINGALE and SKYTRAIN II (USA)
First flight 1968

Data: C-9A Nightingale; weights and performance for DC-9 Srs 30

Power plant: Two Pratt & Whitney JT8D-9 turbofan engines (each 14 500 lb; 6 575 kg st)

Wing span: 93 ft 5 in (28.47 m)

Length overall: 119 ft 3½ in (36.37 m)

Cabin:
Max width 10 ft 1 in (3.07 m)
Max height 6 ft 9 in (2.06 m)

Freight hold (underfloor): 895 cu ft (25.3 m³)

Max weight-limited payload: 26 156 lb (11 864 kg)

Max T-O weight: 98 000 lb (44 450 kg)

Max cruising speed at 25 000 ft (7 620 m): 491 knots (565 mph; 909 km/h)

Range at 30 000 ft (9 150 m), at Mach 0.8, with reserves for 200 nm (230 mile; 370 km) flight to alternate and 60 min hold at 10 000 ft (3 050 m): 1 288 nm (1 484 miles; 2 388 km)

Accommodation: C-9A can carry 30 to 40 stretchers, more than 40 ambulatory patients or a combination of the two, together with two nurses and three aeromedical technicians

Ordered by: Air forces of Italy (2 DC-9-32) and USA (Air Force 21 C-9A; Navy 8 C-9B)

NATO Code Names *Fagot* (MiG-15) and *Midget* (MiG-15UTI)

Fighter (MiG-15) and operational trainer (MiG-15UTI)

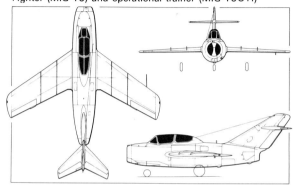

Photo and drawing: MiG-15UTI

Data: MiG-15bis

Power plant: One Klimov VK-1 turbojet engine (5 950 lb; 2 700 kg st)

Wing span: 33 ft 0¾ in (10.08 m)

Length overall: 33 ft 1¾ in (10.10 m)

T-O weights:
clean 10 935 lb (4 960 kg)
normal max 12 756 lb (5 786 kg)
overload max 14 242 lb (6 460 kg)

Max level speed at 39 375 ft (12 000 m): 580 knots (668 mph; 1 076 km/h)

Max rate of climb at S/L: 10 400 ft (3 170 m)/min

MIKOYAN/GUREVICH MiG-15 and MiG-15UTI (USSR)
First flights 1947/1950

Service ceiling: 50 850 ft (15 500 m)

Range:
internal fuel, AUW of 4 960 kg 653 nm (752 miles; 1 210 km)
internal fuel, AUW of 5 786 kg 1 003 nm (1 155 miles; 1 860 km)
max, with auxiliary tanks 1 080 nm (1 243 miles; 2 000 km)

Accommodation: Pilot, on ejection seat. Two seats in tandem in MiG-15UTI.

Armament: One 37 mm N-37 cannon, with 40 rds, under nose on starboard side, and two 23 mm NR-23 cannon, each with 80 rds, under nose on port side. Underwing attachments for two 100, 250 or 500 kg bombs, rockets, or two 88 Imp gallon (400 litre) drop-tanks

Ordered by:

MiG-15: Albania (20), Algeria (20), China (500), Cuba (20), Czechoslovakia (S-102/3), Egypt (30), Indonesia (10), North Korea (15), Mali (few), Mongolia (6), Poland (LiM-2), Romania, Somalia (6), and USSR

MiG-15UTI: Afghanistan (6), Albania, Algeria, Bulgaria (20), China, Cuba (30), Czechoslovakia (CS-102), Egypt, Finland (3), German Democratic Republic, Hungary, Indonesia, Iraq, Khmer (3), North Korea, Mali (1), Mongolia, Pakistan (4), Poland (LiM-1), Romania, Somalia (6), Sri Lanka (1), Syria, Uganda (2), USSR and North Vietnam

All quantities represent estimated numbers in service not original orders

NATO Code Name *Hare*
Light general-purpose helicopter

MIL Mi-1/ Mi-3 (USSR)
First flights 1948/1956

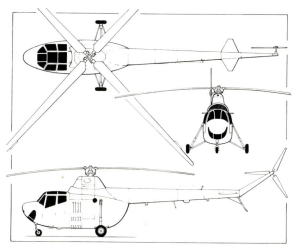

Photo and drawing: Mi-1

Data: SM-1W

Power plant: One LiT-3 (Polish-built AI-26V) seven-cylinder radial piston engine (575 hp)

Main rotor diameter: 47 ft 1 in (14.35 m)

Length of fuselage: 39 ft 8½ in (12.10 m)

Max T-O weight: 5 425 lb (2 460 kg)

Max level speed at S/L: 92 knots (106 mph; 170 km/h)

Max rate of climb at 2 000 ft (610 m) altitude at AUW of 5 070 lb (2 300 kg): 1 043 ft (318 m)/min

Service ceiling: 9 840 ft (3 000 m)

Max range at econ cruising speed at 3 280 ft (1 000 m): 321 nm (370 miles; 600 km)

Accommodation: Pilot, and three passengers or freight. Ambulance version (SM-1WS) accommodates pilot, two stretchers and attendant. In the dual-control trainer (SM-1WSZ), the instructor is seated in the rear of the cabin. Space for up to 132 lb (60 kg) of baggage

Ordered by: Air forces of Afghanistan, Albania (3 or 4), Algeria (3), Bulgaria (SM-1), China, Cuba (20), Czechoslovakia, Egypt, Finland, Hungary, Iraq, North Korea, Mongolia, Poland (SM-1), Syria (4), USSR and Yemen. All quantities estimated

Liaison and reconnaissance/support (MU-2C), search and rescue (MU-2E and K) and flight calibration (MU-2J) aircraft

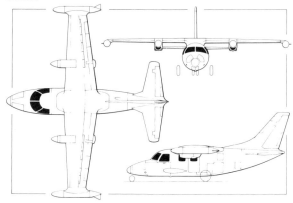

Photo and drawing: LR-1 (MU-2C)

Data: LR-1 (MU-2C)

Power plant: Two AiResearch TPE-331-25A turboprop engines (each 605 ehp)

Wing span over tip-tanks: 39 ft 2 in (11.95 m)

Length overall: 33 ft 3 in (10.13 m) (MU-2E 35 ft 1¼ in; 10.70 m)

Cabin:

Length 11 ft 0 in (3.34 m)

Max width 4 ft 11 in (1.50 m)

Max height 4 ft 3¼ in (1.30 m)

Max T-O weight: 8 930 lb (4 050 kg)

Max cruising speed at 10 000 ft (3 050 m): 269 knots (310 mph; 499 km/h)

Max rate of climb at S/L: 2 450 ft (747 m)/min

Service ceiling: 26 500 ft (8 075 m)

Max range, with wingtip tanks, with 30 min reserve: 1 040 nm (1 200 miles; 1 930 km)

Equipment (LR-1): One vertical and one swing-type oblique camera in photographic version. One aircraft with infra-red radar, and one with no wingtip tanks. Optional equipment includes infra-red photographic equipment or side-looking airborne radar. MU-2E has Doppler radar in extended "thimble" nose, extra fuel, bulged observation window each side of fuselage, and provision for dropping a lifeboat via a sliding door in fuselage

Ordered by: Japan (Air Force 16 MU-2E, 4 MU-2J and 8 MU-2K; Army 9 MU-2C/LR-1)

Supersonic trainer (T-2) and close-support fighter (FS-T2-KAI)

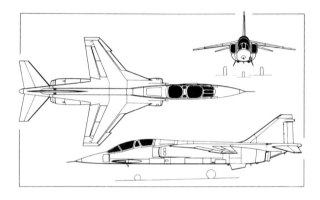

Photo and drawing: T-2

MITSUBISHI T-2 and FS-T2-KAI (Japan)
First flight 1971

Data: T-2
Power plant: Two Rolls-Royce/Turboméca Adour turbofan engines (each 7 140 lb; 3 238 kg st with afterburning)
Wing span: 25 ft 10 in (7.87 m)
Length overall: 58 ft 7 in (17.86 m)
Max T-O weight, clean: 21 274 lb (9 650 kg)
Max level speed at 36 000 ft (11 000 m), clean: Mach 1.6
Service ceiling, clean: 50 025 ft (15 250 m)
Max ferry range with external tanks: 1 550 nm (1 785 miles; 2 870 km)
Accommodation: Crew of two in tandem on Weber ES-7J zero-zero ejection seats. FS-T2-KAI flown as single-seater
Armament: One Vulcan multi-barrel 20 mm cannon in lower fuselage, aft of cockpit on port side. Attachment point on under-fuselage centreline and two under each wing for drop-tanks or other stores. Wingtip attachments on both versions for air-to-air missiles; FS-T2-KAI can carry two or four air-to-air missiles, eight to twelve 500 lb bombs, or rockets, on wing and fuselage hardpoints
Ordered by: Japan (Air Force 59 T-2 and 68 FS-T2-KAI)

Training, communications/liaison, photographic and light attack aircraft

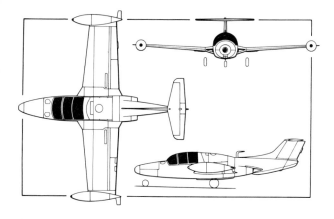

MORANE-SAULNIER 760 PARIS
(France)
First flight 1954

Data: Paris I (MS 760A)

Power plant: Two Turboméca Marboré IIC turbojet engines (each 880 lb; 400 kg st)

Wing span (over tip-tanks): 33 ft 3 in (10.13 m)

Length overall: 33 ft 7 in (10.24 m)

Max T-O weight: 7 650 lb (3 470 kg)

Max level speed at S/L: 352 knots (405 mph; 652 km/h)

Max rate of climb at S/L: 2 264 ft (680 m)/min

Max range at 22 975 ft (7 000 m), with reserves: 807 nm (930 miles; 1 500 km)

Accommodation: Seating for up to four persons, including pilot. Dual controls in training version

Armament (optional): As trainer, two 7.5 mm machine-guns and four 3.5 in rockets or two 50 kg bombs. In single-seat light attack configuration, one 30 mm cannon and two 7.5 mm machine-guns and either eight 50 kg or two 50 kg and two 120 kg bombs

Ordered by: Air forces of Argentine (48 MS 760A), France (Air Force approx 50 MS 760A; Navy 15 MS 760B) and Paraguay (1 MS 760B)

Short-range VIP, troop and freight transport, and anti-submarine trainer

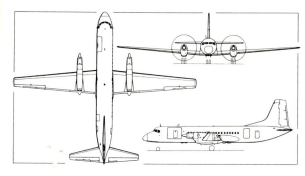

Drawing: YS-11A-300/600

Data: YS-11A-200
Power plant: Two Rolls-Royce Dart RDa.10/1 Mk 542-10K turboprop engines (each 3 060 ehp)
Wing span: 104 ft 11¾ in (32.00 m)
Length overall: 86 ft 3½ in (26.30 m)

Cabin, excl flight deck, galley and toilets:
 Length 44 ft 1 in (13.44 m)
 Max width 8 ft 10 in (2.70 m)
 Max height 6 ft 6 in (1.99 m)
 Volume 2 150 cu ft (61.00 m³)
Baggage compartment (fwd of cabin): 94 cu ft (2.66 m³)
Freight holds:
 aft of cabin 213 cu ft (6.03 m³)
 under floor 70 cu ft (1.98 m³)
Max payload: 14 508 lb (6 581 kg)
Max T-O weight: 54 010 lb (24 500 kg)
Max cruising speed at 15 000 ft (4 575 m): 253 knots (291 mph; 469 km/h)
Max rate of climb at S/L: 1 220 ft (372 m)/min
Service ceiling: 22 900 ft (6 980 m)
Range with max fuel, no reserves:
 with bag tanks 1 736 nm (2 000 miles; 3 215 km)
 without bag tanks 1 137 nm (1 310 miles; 2 110 km)
Range with max payload, no reserves: 590 nm (680 miles; 1 090 km)
Accommodation: Flight crew of two and up to 60 passengers. Freight hold aft cabin. Baggage compartment forward of cabin, second freight hold under floor, forward of wings
Ordered by: Japan (Air Force 4 YS-11-100, 1 YS-11A-200, 1 YS-11A-300 and 7 YS-11A-400; Navy 1 YS-11-100, 4 YS-11A-200 and 2 YS-11A-400)

Utility (C-42) and liaison/observation aircraft (L-42)

NEIVA C-42/L-42 REGENTE (Brazil)
First flight 1961

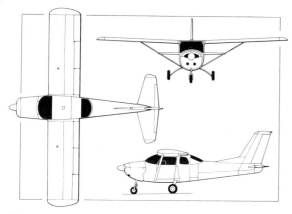

Photo and drawing: L-42 Regente

Data: L-42 Regente
Power plant: One Continental IO-360-D six-cylinder piston engine (210 hp)
Wing span: 29 ft 11½ in (9.13 m)
Length overall: 23 ft 7¾ in (7.21 m)
Cabin:
  Max length 6 ft 6¾ in (2.00 m)
  Max width 3 ft 3¼ in (1.00 m)
  Max height 3 ft 11¼ in (1.20 m)
  Volume 219 cu ft (6.20 m³)
Max T-O weight: 2 293 lb (1 040 kg)
Max level speed at S/L: 132 knots (153 mph; 246 km/h)
Max rate of climb at S/L: 918 ft (280 m)/min
Service ceiling: 15 810 ft (4 820 m)
Range with max payload, no reserves: 498 nm (574 miles; 925 km)
Accommodation: Pilot and co-pilot/doctor, with third seat at rear for navigator/observer. Rear compartment for up to 40 lb (18 kg) of baggage. Dual controls standard
Ordered by: Brazilian Air Force (80 C-42 and 40 L-42)

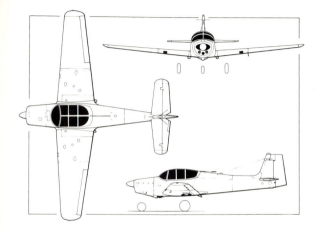

NEIVA T-25 UNIVERSAL (Brazil)
First flight 1966

Data: T-25 (Utility category)

Power plant: One Lycoming IO-540-K1D5 six-cylinder piston engine (300 hp)

Wing span: 36 ft 1 in (11.00 m)

Length overall: 28 ft 2½ in (8.60 m)

Cabin:
Length 7 ft 2½ in (2.20 m)
Max width 4 ft 1 in (1.25 m)
Max height 4 ft 1 in (1.25 m)
Volume 141 cu ft (4.00 m³)

Baggage compartment volume: 12.5 cu ft (0.35 m³)

Max T-O weight: 3 747 lb (1 700 kg)

Max level speed at S/L: 160 knots (184 mph; 296 km/h)

Max rate of climb at S/L: 1 050 ft (320 m)/min

Service ceiling: 16 400 ft (5 000 m)

Range (75% power) at 6 550 ft (2 000 m), 10% reserves: 809 nm (932 miles; 1 500 km)

Accommodation: Two seats side by side, with dual controls; optional third seat at rear. Baggage compartment aft of rear seat

Ordered by: Brazilian Air Force (150); tandem two-seat light attack version, named Carajá, reported under development, with 400 hp Lycoming engine, two wing-mounted 7.62 mm guns and underwing hardpoints

Short/medium-range troop and freight transport (N 2501/2) and anti-submarine warfare trainer (N 2504)

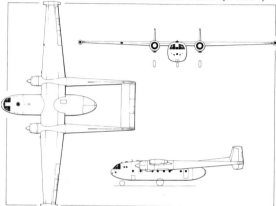

Photo: Nord 2501 flying classroom
Drawing: Nord 2504

Data: N 2501
Power plant: Two SNECMA-built Bristol Hercules 738 or 758 fourteen-cylinder radial piston engines (each 2 040 hp)

NORD NORATLAS (France)
First flight 1950

Wing span: 106 ft 7½ in (32.50 m)
Length overall: 72 ft 0½ in (21.96 m)
Cabin (excl flight deck and rear doors):
  Length 32 ft 5¾ in (9.90 m)
  Max width 9 ft 0¼ in (2.75 m)
  Max height 7 ft 10½ in (2.40 m)
Normal max T-O weight: 45 415 lb (20 600 kg)
Max overload T-O weight: 48 500 lb (22 000 kg)
Max level speed at 5 000 ft (1 525 m): 218.5 knots (251 mph; 405 km/h)
Max cruising speed at 9 850 ft (3 000 m): 181 knots (208 mph; 335 km/h)
Max rate of climb at S/L: 1 180 ft (360 m)/min
Service ceiling: 23 300 ft (7 100 m)
Range with 11 025 lb (5 000 kg) payload: 1 346 nm (1 550 miles; 2 500 km)
Range with max payload: 809 nm (932 miles; 1 500 km)
Accommodation: Crew of five and up to 45 troops/paratroops. Alternative accommodation for stretchers, wheeled vehicles or up to 14 990 lb (6 800 kg) of freight
Ordered by: Air forces of Chad (1 or 2 N 2501), France (Air Force 200 N 2501; Navy 5 N 2504), German Federal Republic (186 N 2501D and 2 N 2508), Greece (approx 40 ex-German N 2501D), Israel (30 N 2501), Niger (4 ex-German N 2501D) and Portugal (12 N 2501, approx 10 ex-German N 2501D, and 6 N 2502)

Counter-insurgency fighter

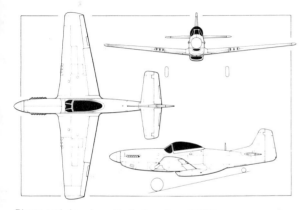

Photo and drawing: North American F-51D

NORTH AMERICAN / CAVALIER F-51D
MUSTANG (USA)
First flights / 1940 1967

Data: Cavalier F-51D Mustang

Power plant: One Packard V-1650-7 (Rolls-Royce Merlin) twelve-cylinder Vee piston engine (1 695 hp)

Wing span: 37 ft 0½ in (11.28 m)

Length overall: 32 ft 2½ in (9.81 m)

Max T-O weight: 12 500 lb (5 670 kg)

Max level speed: 397 knots (457 mph; 735 km/h)

Max range at 252 knots (290 mph; 466 km/h): 1 720 nm (1 980 miles; 3 185 km)

Accommodation: Crew of two in tandem

Armament: Standard fixed armament of six 0.50 in machine-guns, three in each wing. Four hardpoints under each wing, each inboard point able to carry a 1 000 lb bomb or 110 US gallon (415 litre) fuel tank. The other six hardpoints carry 5 in air-to-surface rockets. The TF-51D training version has only four guns in the wings

Ordered by: Air forces of Bolivia (12 Cavalier F-51D), Dominica (approx 20), El Salvador (6 Cavalier F-51D), Guatemala (10), Haiti (6) and Indonesia (10)

Basic trainer and light attack aircraft

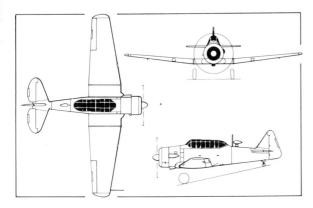

Photo and drawing: T-6G (Spanish E-16)

NORTH AMERICAN T-6 TEXAN (USA)
First flight 1938

Data: T-6G Texan

Power plant: One Pratt & Whitney R-1340-AN-1 nine-cylinder radial piston engine (550 hp)

Wing span: 42 ft 0 in (12.80 m)

Length overall: 29 ft 6 in (8.99 m)

Max T-O weight: 5 617 lb (2 548 kg)

Max level speed at 5 000 ft (1 525 m): 184 knots (212 mph; 341 km/h)

Max rate of climb at S/L: 1 643 ft (501 m)/min

Service ceiling: 24 750 ft (7 543 m)

Normal range: 755 nm (870 miles; 1 400 km)

Accommodation: Two seats in tandem

Armament: Underwing attachments for light bombs and rockets

Ordered by: Air forces of Argentine (Navy 6 SNJ-5), Bolivia (18 SNJ-6, 5 T-6G), Brazil (30 T-6G), Chile (6 T-6), Dominica (T-6), Ecuador (T-6), Greece (20 T-6D/G), Guatemala (7 T-6), Haiti (3 T-6), Honduras (3 T-6), India (160 T-6G), Indonesia (T-6G), Iran (T-6), Israel (T-6), Italy (T-6C/D/F/G), Khmer (6 T-6G), Laos (10 T-6), Mexico (45 AT-6), Morocco (50 T-6), New Zealand (19 T-6), Nicaragua (4 T-6), Pakistan (30 T-6G), Paraguay (14 T-6), Peru (15 T-6), Portugal (288 T-6), South Africa (100 T-6), Spain (200 T-6D/G), Taiwan (T-6), Thailand (140 T-6), Tunisia (12 T-6), Turkey (40 CCF Harvard), Uruguay (Air Force 10 T-6; Navy 3 SNJ), UK (3 Harvard), Venezuela (T-6) and Zaire (32 T-6G). Quantities in most cases represent approx numbers in service, not original orders

NORTHROP T-38A TALON (USA)
First flight 1959

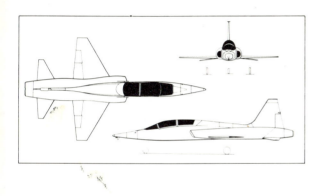

Power plant: Two General Electric J85-GE-5 turbojet engines (each 3 850 lb; 1 748 kg st with afterburning)
Wing span: 25 ft 3 in (7.70 m)
Length overall: 46 ft 4½ in (14.13 m)
Max T-O weight: 12 093 lb (5 485 kg)
Max level speed (50% fuel) at 36 000 ft (11 000 m): above Mach 1.23
Max rate of climb at S/L (50% fuel): 30 000 ft (9 145 m)/min
Service ceiling (50% fuel): 53 600 ft (16 335 m)
Range with max fuel, with reserve fuel for 20 min max endurance at sea level:
  crew of two 950 nm (1 093 miles; 1 759 km)
  crew of one 980 nm (1 128 miles; 1 815 km)
Accommodation: Pupil and instructor in tandem on rocket-powered ejection seats
Ordered by: US Air Force (1 187, incl 46 for German Air Force, 24 for NASA and 5 for US Navy)

Primary trainer

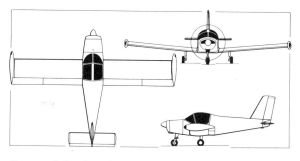

Photo and drawing: PL-1B

Data: AIDC/Pazmany PL-1B Chienshou
Power plant: One Lycoming O-320-E2A four-cylinder piston engine (150 hp)
Wing span: 28 ft 0 in (8.53 m)
Length overall: 19 ft 8⅛ in (5.99 m)
Cabin:
   Length 4 ft 2 in (1.27 m)
   Max width 3 ft 6½ in (1.07 m)
   Max height 3 ft 4 in (1.02 m)
Max T-O weight: 1 440 lb (653 kg)
Max level speed at S/L: 130 knots (150 mph; 241 km/h)
Max rate of climb at S/L: 1 600 ft (488 m)/min
Range with max fuel: 350 nm (405 miles; 650 km)
Accommodation: Two seats side by side. Dual controls. Space for 40 lb (18 kg) baggage aft of seats
Ordered by: Air forces of South Korea (4 PL-2), Taiwan (Air Force 3 PL-1A, 40 PL-1B; Army 10 PL-1B), Thailand (2 PL-2) and South Vietnam (1 PL-2)

PIAGGIO P.148 (Italy)
First flight 1951

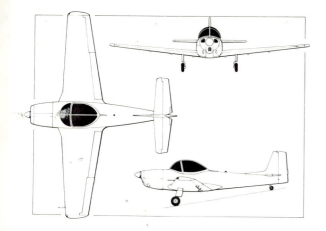

Power plant: One Lycoming 0-435-A six-cylinder piston engine (190 hp)
Wing span: 36 ft 5¾ in (11.12 m)
Length overall: 27 ft 8½ in (8.45 m)
Max T-O weight (two-seat): 2 645 lb (1 200 kg)
Max level speed at S/L (two-seat): 127 knots (146 mph; 235 km/h)
Max rate of climb at S/L: 900 ft (275 m)/min
Service ceiling (two-seat): 16 400 ft (5 000 m)
Range, including start, warm-up, take-off and climb: 498 nm (573 miles; 923 km)
Accommodation: Two seats side by side, with dual controls. Optional third seat aft
Ordered by: Air forces of Italy (100) and Zaïre (12, ex-Italian Air Force)

PIAGGIO P.149 (Italy)
First flight 1953

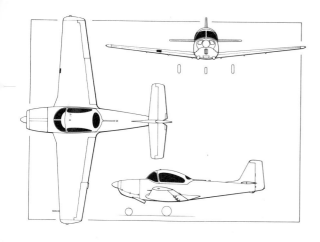

Data: P.149D

Power plant: One Lycoming GO-480 six-cylinder piston engine (270 hp)

Wing span: 36 ft 5¾ in (11.12 m)

Length overall: 28 ft 9½ in (8.78 m)

Max T-O weight: 3 704 lb (1 680 kg)

Max level speed at S/L: 167 knots (192 mph; 309 km/h)

Max rate of climb at S/L: 980 ft (300 m)/min

Service ceiling: 19 850 ft (6 050 m)

Range, incl allowance for starting, warm-up, take-off and climb, plus 30 min reserve, at 10 825 ft (3 300 m): 590 nm (680 miles; 1 095 km)

Accommodation: Pilot and pupil/co-pilot/passenger on front seats, and up to 3 passengers at rear. Dual controls. Large baggage compartment behind rear seat

Ordered by: Air forces of German Federal Republic (262 P.149D), Nigeria (26 ex-German P.149D), Tanzania (5 ex-German P.149D) and Uganda (10 P.149U)

Light transport, training, ambulance, communications, search/surveillance and coastal patrol aircraft

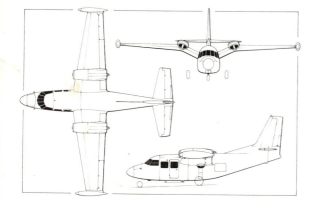

Data: P.166M
Power plant: Two Lycoming GSO-480-B1C6 six-cylinder piston engines (each 340 hp)
Wing span: 46 ft 9 in (14.25 m)
Length overall: 38 ft 1 in (11.60 m)
Max T-O weight: 8 115 lb (3 680 kg)
Max level speed at 9 500 ft (2 900 m): 193 knots (222 mph; 357 km/h)
Max rate of climb at S/L: 1 240 ft (380 m)/min
Service ceiling: 25 500 ft (7 770 m)
Range (at 55% power), including allowances for starting, warm-up, taxying, take-off, climb, descent and 30 min reserve, at 15 000 ft (4 550 m): 1 042 nm (1 200 miles; 1 930 km)
Accommodation: Seating for up to ten persons, including pilot. Alternative layouts provide for ambulance, training, communications or freight-carrying duties
Ordered by: Air forces of Italy (51 P.166M and 20 P.166S) and South Africa (9 P.166M Albatross); ASW, para-dropping and armed versions under development

Light transport (PD-808 VIP and PD-808 TA), navigation trainer (PD-808 TA) and ECM aircraft (PD-808 ECM)

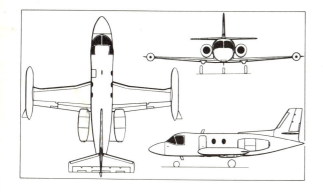

PIAGGIO PD-808 (Italy)
First flight 1964

Data: Civil PD-808 526 (military PD-808 VIP generally similar)

Power plant: Two Rolls-Royce Bristol Viper Mk 526 turbojet engines (each 3 360 lb; 1 524 kg st)

Wing span: 37 ft 6 in (11.43 m)

Length overall: 42 ft 2 in (12.85 m)

Cabin:
Length 14 ft 8 in (4.47 m)
Max width 5 ft 4½ in (1.64 m)
Max height 4 ft 9 in (1.45 m)
Volume 291 cu ft (8.24 m³)

Max payload: 1 600 lb (726 kg)

Max T-O weight: 18 000 lb (8 165 kg)

Max level speed at 19 500 ft (5 945 m): 460 knots (529 mph; 852 km/h)

Max rate of climb at S/L at AUW of 15 821 lb (7 176 kg): 5 400 ft (1 650 m)/min

Service ceiling: 45 000 ft (13 715 m)

Range with max fuel and 840 lb (381 kg) payload, 45 min reserve: 1 148 nm (1 322 miles; 2 128 km)

Accommodation: Flight crew of one or two. Six seats in VIP version, nine in transport and navigation training versions. The navigation training version has one main student station in the co-pilot's seat, with two or three more student stations in cabin. Electronic countermeasures version accommodates two pilots and three equipment operators

Ordered by: Italy (armed forces 2 prototypes and 25 PD-808 VIP/TA/ECM)

PILATUS P-3 (Switzerland)
First flight 1953

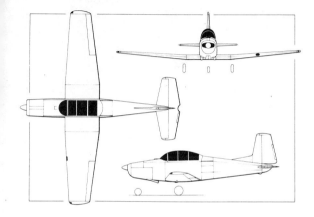

Power plant: One Lycoming GO-435-C2A six-cylinder piston engine (260 hp)

Wing span: 34 ft 1 in (10.40 m)

Length overall: 28 ft 8½ in (8.75 m)

Max permissible loaded weight: 3 300 lb (1 500 kg)

Max level speed at S/L: 167 knots (193 mph; 310 km/h)

Max rate of climb at S/L: 1 378 ft (420 m)/min

Service ceiling: 18 050 ft (5 500 m)

Max range: 404 nm (466 miles; 750 km)

Accommodation: Crew of two in tandem with dual controls

Armament (weapon training role): One 7.9 mm machine-gun with 180 rds, in pod under port wing; two underwing racks for four 12 kg practice bombs or two 5 cm rockets

Ordered by: Brazil (Air Force/Navy 6) and Swiss Air Force (72)

STOL utility transport (Porter/Turbo-Porter) and light tactical support aircraft (Peacemaker)

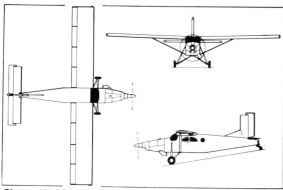

Photo: AU-23A Peacemaker **Drawing:** PC-6/A Turbo-Porter
Data: PC-6/B2-H2 Turbo-Porter
Power plant: One Pratt & Whitney (UACL) PT6A-27 turboprop engine (550 shp); AU-23A has AiResearch TPE 331-1-101F (T76) turboprop of 665 shp
Wing span: 49 ft 8 in (15.13 m)
Length overall: 36 ft 1 in (11.00 m)
Cabin, from back of pilot's seat to rear wall:
Length 7 ft 6½ in (2.30 m)
Max width 3 ft 9½ in (1.16 m)
Max height (at front) 4 ft 2½ in (1.28 m)
Volume 107 cu ft (3.28 m³)
Max T-O weight: 4 850 lb (2 200 kg)

PILATUS PORTER and TURBO-PORTER and FAIRCHILD INDUSTRIES AU-23A PEACEMAKER (Switzerland/USA)
First flights 1959/1961/1970

Max cruising speed at 10 000 ft (3 050 m): 140 knots (161 mph; 259 km/h)
Max rate of climb at S/L: 1 580 ft (482 m)/min
Service ceiling: 30 025 ft (9 150 m)
Max range with max internal fuel and two 190 litre drop-tanks: 875 nm (1 006 miles; 1 620 km)
Accommodation: Pilot and up to nine passengers. Seats quickly removable for freight carrying. Hatch in floor for installation of aerial camera or for supply dropping. Hatch in cabin rear wall permits stowage of six passenger seats or accommodation of freight items up to 16 ft 5 in (5.0 m) in length. Dual controls optional
Armament (Fairchild Industries Peacemaker only): One underfuselage hardpoint capable of carrying a 590 lb (268 kg) store, and four underwing hardpoints, of which the inboard pair can carry 510 lb (231 kg) each, and the outboard pair 350 lb (159 kg) each. However, total external load on each wing may not exceed 700 lb (318 kg). Armament and equipment carried on the hardpoints can include gun or rocket pods, bombs, a broadcasting pod, cameras and flare dispensers. Two side-firing Miniguns or XM-197 20 mm guns in cabin
Ordered by: Air forces of Australia (Army 19 Turbo-Porter), Colombia (6 Porter/Turbo-Porter), Ecuador (2 Turbo-Porter), Israel (2 Turbo-Porter), Peru (1 Turbo-Porter), Sudan (8 Turbo-Porter), Switzerland (12 Porter and 15 Turbo-Porter), and USA (15 Peacemaker, of which 13 supplied to Royal Thai Air Force)

Utility transport

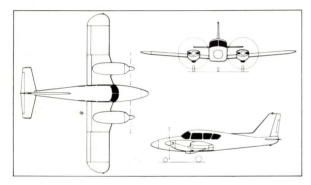

Photo and drawing: Turbo Aztec E (Spanish E-19)

Data: Turbo Aztec E

Power plant: Two Lycoming TIO-540-C1A six-cylinder piston engines (each 250 hp)

Wing span: 37 ft 2½ in (11.34 m)

Length overall: 31 ft 2¾ in (9.52 m)

Baggage compartments:
front 21.3 cu ft (0.60 m^3)
rear 25.4 cu ft (0.72 m^3)

Max T-O weight: 5 200 lb (2 360 kg)

Max level speed at 18 500 ft (5 639 m): 220 knots (253 mph; 407 km/h)

Max rate of climb at S/L: 1 530 ft (466 m)/min

Absolute ceiling: over 30 000 ft (9 145 m)

Range with max fuel at 170 knots (196 mph; 315 km/h) at 24 000 ft (7 315 m): 1 137 nm (1 310 miles; 2 108 km)

Accommodation: Seating for six persons, including pilot. Dual controls standard. Provision for carrying stretcher, survey camera or freight. Baggage compartments at rear of cabin and in nose

Ordered by: Air forces of France (2 Aztec), Spain (2 Aztec and 6 Turbo Aztec E) and USA (Navy 20 U-11A Aztec)

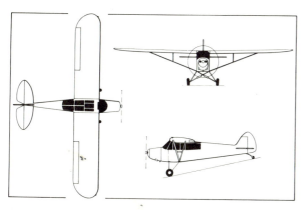

Photo and drawing: U-7 Super Cub

Data: U-7A
Power plant: One Lycoming O-290-11 four-cylinder piston engine (125 hp)
Wing span: 35 ft 3 in (10.73 m)
Length overall: 22 ft 7 in (6.88 m)
Max T-O weight: 1 580 lb (717 kg)
Max level speed: 107 knots (123 mph; 198 km/h)
Max rate of climb at S/L: 1 000 ft (305 m)/min
Service ceiling: 21 650 ft (6 600 m)
Range: 668 nm (770 miles; 1 240 km)
Accommodation: Two seats in tandem
Ordered by: Air forces of Belgium (Army 4 L-18C), Denmark (Army 2 L-18C), France (Army 12 L-18C/L-21A), Greece (Army 20 L-21A), Indonesia (Air Force few L-4J), Iran (Army L-18C), Israel (Air Force 60 L-18C), Italy (Air Force 50 L-18/L-21A), Norway (Air Force 24 L-18C), Paraguay (Air Force 4 L-4A), Portugal (27 L-21B), Switzerland (Army L-18), Turkey (Army 80 L-18B), Uganda (Air Force 16 L-18C), Uruguay (Air Force 3 L-21A) and USA (Air Force 243 civil PA-18, 120 L-21A/U-7A and 582 L-21B/U-7B; Army 838 L-18C and 30 L-21A/U-7A). Procurement figures given for US Air Force Army; other quantities are approx numbers in service, not original orders

STOL general-purpose aircraft

Photo and drawing: Wilga 35

PZL-104 WILGA/GELATIK 32 (Poland/Indonesia)

First flight 1962

Data: Wilga 35
Power plant: One Ivchenko AI-14R nine-cylinder radial piston engine (260 hp)
Wing span: 36 ft 4⅞ in (11.14 m)
Length overall: 26 ft 6¾ in (8.10 m)
Cabin:
  Length 7 ft 2½ in (2.20 m)
  Max width 3 ft 10 in (1.20 m)
  Max height 4 ft 11 in (1.50 m)
  Volume 85 cu ft (2.40 m³)
Baggage compartment: 17.5 cu ft (0.50 m³)
Max T-O weight: 2 755 lb (1 250 kg)
Max level speed: 108 knots (125 mph; 201 km/h)
Max rate of climb at S/L: 1 245 ft (380 m)/min
Service ceiling: 15 025 ft (4 580 m)
Range with max fuel, 30 min reserve: 366 nm (422 miles; 680 km)
Accommodation: Seating for 4 persons in two pairs. Baggage compartment aft of seats. Parachute training version has the starboard door removed and replaced by two tubular uprights with a central connecting strap, and the starboard front seat is rearward-facing. Ambulance versions also available
Ordered by: Air forces of Indonesia (56 Gelatik) and Poland

Liaison, training and general purpose transport aircraft

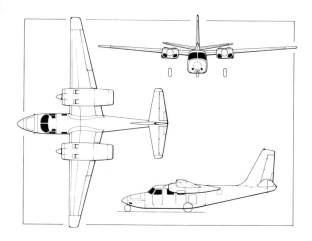

Photo and drawing: Shrike Commander

Data: Standard Shrike Commander
Power plant: Two Lycoming IO-540-E1B5 six-cylinder piston engines (each 290 hp)
Wing span: 49 ft 0½ in (14.95 m)
Length overall: 36 ft 9¾ in (11.22 m)

ROCKWELL COMMANDER, SHRIKE COMMANDER and TURBO COMMANDER (USA)
First flights 1958/1969/1964

Cabin:
Length 10 ft 7½ in (3.24 m)
Max width 4 ft 4 in (1.32 m)
Max height 4 ft 5 in (1.35 m)
Volume 177 cu ft (5.01 m³)
Baggage hold: 33 cu ft (0.93 m³)
Max T-O weight: 6 750 lb (3 062 kg)
Cruising speed (75% power) at 9 000 ft (2 745 m):
176 knots (203 mph; 326 km/h) TAS
Max rate of climb at S/L: 1 340 ft (408 m)/min
Service ceiling: 19 400 ft (5 913 m)
Range with standard fuel at 9 000 ft (2 745 m) at 178 knots (205 mph; 330 km/h) TAS:
45 min reserve 693 nm (798 miles; 1 284 km)
no reserve 824 nm (948 miles; 1 525 km)
Accommodation: Seating for up to seven persons, including one or two pilots; two front positions have dual controls. Cabin can be used for freight carrying. Compartment for 500 lb (227 kg) baggage aft of cabin
Ordered by: Air forces of Argentine (14 Shrike Commander), Colombia (1 Aero Commander 560A), Dahomey (1 Aero Commander 500B), Dominica (1 Aero Commander 500), Greece (2 Aero Commander 680FL), Guatemala (1 Turbo Commander), Indonesia (Navy 3 Grand Commander), Iran (3 Turbo Commander), Ivory Coast (1 Aero Commander 500), Kenya (1 Turbo Commander), Laos (4 Aero Commander 520), Pakistan (1 Aero Commander), Philippines (1 Aero Commander 520) and USA (Air Force 15 U-4A and U-4B; Army 1 U-9B, 4 U-9C and 2 RU-9D)

General-purpose trainer

ROCKWELL INTERNATIONAL T-2
BUCKEYE (USA)
First flight 1958

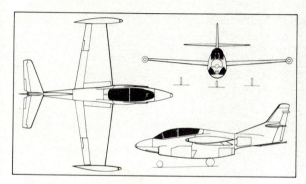

Photo: T-2B

Data: T-2C
Power plant: Two General Electric J85-GE-4 turbojet
engines (each 2 950 lb; 1 339 kg st)
Wing span over tip-tanks: 38 ft 1½ in (11.62 m)
Length overall: 38 ft 3½ in (11.67 m)
Max T-O weight: 13 179 lb (5 977 kg)
Max level speed at 25 000 ft (7 620 m): 453 knots
(522 mph; 840 km/h)
Max rate of climb at S/L: 6 200 ft (1 890 m)/min
Service ceiling: 40 425 ft (12 320 m)
Max range: 909 nm (1 047 miles; 1 685 km)
Accommodation: Pupil and instructor in tandem on
rocket-powered LS-1 ejection seats
Armament: Optional packaged installations of guns,
target towing gear, 100 lb practice bombs, M-5 or
MK76 practice bomb clusters, Aero 4B practice bomb
containers, 2.25 in rocket launchers or seven 2.75 in
rockets in Aero 6A-1 rocket containers, can be carried
on underwing store stations, one beneath each wing,
with a combined capacity of 640 lb (290 kg)
Ordered by: USA (Navy 97 T-2B and 183 T-2C) and
Venezuela (12 T-2D)

Aircrew trainer

ROCKWELL (NORTH AMERICAN) T-39 SABRE (USA)
First flight 1958

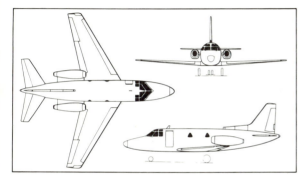

Photo: CT-39E
Drawing: T-39A

Data: Sabre Series 40 (CT-39E similar)
Power plant: Two Pratt & Whitney JT12A-8 turbojet engines (each 3 300 lb; 1 497 kg st)
Wing span: 44 ft 5¼ in (13.54 m)
Length overall: 43 ft 9 in (13.34 m)
Cabin, excluding flight deck:
Length 16 ft 0 in (4.88 m)
Max width 5 ft 2½ in (1.59 m)
Max height 5 ft 7½ in (1.71 m)
Volume 400 cu ft (11.33 m³)
Max payload, incl crew: 2 000 lb (907 kg)
Max T-O weight: 18 650 lb (8 498 kg)
Max level speed at 21 500 ft (6 550 m): 489 knots (563 mph; 906 km/h)
Max rate of climb at S/L: 4 800 ft (1 463 m)/min
Operational ceiling at AUW of 16 000 lb (7 257 kg): 45 000 ft (13 700 m)
Best range, with 4 passengers, baggage, max fuel and 45 min reserve: 1 840 nm (2 118 miles; 3 408 km)
Accommodation: Crew of two and up to nine passengers. Baggage space at front of cabin. With seats removed there is room for 2 500 lb (1 135 kg) of freight
Ordered by: USA (Air Force 143 T-39A, of which 3 cvtd to T-39F, and 6 T-39B; Navy 42 T-39D and 9 CT-39E)

SCOTTISH AVIATION BULLDOG (UK)
First flight 1969

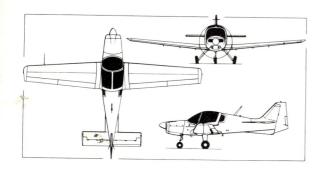

Data: Series 120

Power plant: One Lycoming IO-360-A1B6 four-cylinder piston engine (200 hp)

Wing span: 33 ft 0 in (10.06 m)

Length overall: 23 ft 3 in (7.09 m)

Cabin:
Length 6 ft 11 in (2.11 m)
Max width 3 ft 9 in (1.14 m)
Max height 3 ft 4 in (1.02 m)

Max T-O weight: 2 350 lb (1 066 kg)

Max level speed at S/L: 130 knots (150 mph; 241 km/h)

Max rate of climb at S/L: 1 006 ft (306 m)/min

Service ceiling: 17 000 ft (5 180 m)

Range with max fuel: 540 nm (621 miles; 1 000 km)

Accommodation: Pilot and co-pilot or trainee side by side with dual controls, with space at rear for observer's seat or up to 120 lb (54 kg) of baggage

Armament: Standard aircraft is unarmed, but has provision for installation of machine-guns or other stores beneath wings if required

Ordered by: Air forces of Ghana (6 Model 122), Kenya (5 Model 103), Malaysia (15 Model 102), Nigeria (20 Model 123), Sweden (Air Force 58 Model 101, Army 20 Model 101) and UK (132 Model 121/T. Mk 1)

Aircrew trainer

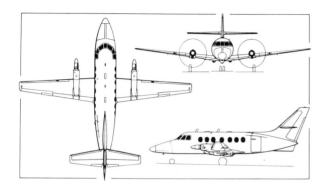

Data: T. Mk 1 (Model 201)
Power plant: Two Turboméca Astazou XVI D turboprop engines (each 996 ehp)
Wing span: 52 ft 0 in (15.85 m)
Length overall: 47 ft 1½ in (14.37 m)
Cabin, excluding flight deck:
Length 24 ft 0 in (7.32 m)
Max width 6 ft 1 in (1.85 m)
Max height 5 ft 11 in (1.80 m)
Volume 638 cu ft (18.05 m³)
Baggage compartment volume (according to layout):
40-60 cu ft (1.13-1.70 m³)
Max payload: 3 814 lb (1 730 kg)
Max T-O weight: 12 566 lb (5 700 kg)
Max level and cruising speed at 10 000 ft (3 050 m):
245 knots (282 mph; 454 km/h)
Max rate of climb at S/L: 2 500 ft (762 m)/min
Service ceiling: 26 000 ft (7 925 m)
Range with max fuel, reserves for 45 min hold and 5% total fuel: 1 200 nm (1 380 miles; 2 224 km)
Accommodation: Pilot and co-pilot or trainee side by side on flight deck, with dual controls, plus four passenger seats in cabin, and toilet
Ordered by: Royal Air Force (26 Model 201/T. Mk 1)

SHORT BELFAST C Mk 1 (UK)
First flight 1964

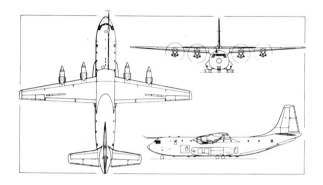

Power plant: Four Rolls-Royce Tyne RTy.12 turboprop engines (each 5 730 ehp)

Wing span: 158 ft 9½ in (48.42 m)

Length overall: 136 ft 5 in (41.69 m)

Hold:
Length, incl ramp 84 ft 4 in (25.70 m)
Max width 16 ft 1 in (4.90 m)
Max height 13 ft 5 in (4.09 m)
Volume 11 000 cu ft (311.5 m³)

Max payload: 78 000 lb (35 400 kg)

Max T-O weight: 230 000 lb (104 300 kg)

Max cruising speed at 200 000 lb (90 720 kg) AUW: 306 knots (352 mph; 566 km/h)

Max rate of climb at S/L: 1 060 ft (323 m)/min

Service ceiling: 30 000 ft (9 145 m)

Range with max fuel, 20% reserve: 4 600 nm (5 300 miles; 8 530 km)

Range with max payload, 20% reserve: 870 nm (1 000 miles; 1 610 km)

Accommodation: Flight crew of four, plus air quartermaster, and freight, including large vehicles, helicopters and guided missiles from strategic offensive missiles to light support weapons. As a troop transport can accommodate up to 250 men

Ordered by: Royal Air Force (10)

STOL utility transport

SHORT SKYVAN Series 3M (UK)
First flight 1963 (3M, 1970)

Power plant: Two AiResearch TPE 331-201 turboprop engines (each 715 shp)
Wing span: 64 ft 11 in (19.79 m)
Length overall, with radome: 41 ft 4 in (12.60 m)
Cabin, excluding flight deck:
Length 18 ft 7 in (5.67 m)
Max width 6 ft 6 in (1.98 m)
Max height 6 ft 6 in (1.98 m)
Volume 780 cu ft (22.09 m³)

Max payload for normal T-O weight: 5 000 lb (2 265 kg)
Max payload for overload T-O weight: 6 000 lb (2 721 kg)
Max T-O weight, normal: 13 700 lb (6 214 kg)
Max T-O weight, overload: 14 500 lb (6 577 kg)
Max cruising speed at 10 000 ft (3 050 m):
max continuous power 176 knots (203 mph; 327 km/h)
cruise power 169 knots (195 mph; 314 km/h)
Max rate of climb at S/L: 1 530 ft (466 m)/min
Service ceiling (100 ft; 30 m/min climb): 22 000 ft (6.705 m)
Range at long-range cruising speed, 45 min reserves, with 293 Imp gallons (1 332 litres) of fuel: 580 nm (670 miles; 1 075 km)
Range (typical freighter) at long-range cruising speed, 45 min reserves, fuel as above, with 5 000 lb (2 268 kg) payload: 208 nm (240 miles; 386 km)
Accommodation: Flight crew of one or two and up to 22 equipped troops or 16 paratroopers and a despatcher. Alternative accommodation for 12 stretchers and two medical attendants or 5 000 lb (2 268 kg) of freight
Ordered by: Air forces of Argentine (Navy 5), Austria (2), Ecuador (Army Air Force 1), Ghana (6), Indonesia (3), Nepal (Army 2), Oman (16), Singapore (6) and Thailand (Police Dept 3)

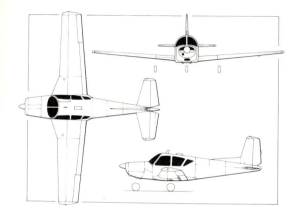

SIAI-MARCHETTI S 208M (Italy)
First flight 1967

Power plant: One Lycoming O-540-E4A5 six-cylinder engine (260 hp)
Wing span: 35 ft 7½ in (10.86 m)
Length overall: 26 ft 3 in (8.00 m)
Cabin:
    Length 5 ft 10¼ in (1.78 m)
    Max width 3 ft 8¾ in (1.14 m)
    Max height 4 ft 4 in (1.32 m)
    Volume 88.0 cu ft (2.50 m³)
Max T-O weight: 3 306 lb (1 500 kg)
Max level speed at S/L: 173 knots (199 mph; 320 km/h)
Max cruising speed: 162 knots (187 mph; 300 km/h)
Range with max internal fuel: 647 nm (746 miles; 1 200 km)
Range with max fuel (incl tip-tanks): 1 085 nm (1 250 miles; 2 000 km)
Accommodation: Seating for pilot and up to four passengers. Baggage compartment aft of seats. Jettisonable cabin door at front on starboard side
Ordered by: Italian Air Force (44)

Trainer (SF.260MX) and light tactical support aircraft (Warrior)

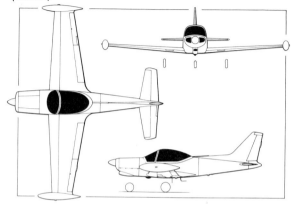

Photo: SF 260W Warrior
Drawing: SF.260M
Data: SF.260MX
Power plant: One Lycoming O-540-E4A5 six-cylinder piston engine (260 hp)
Wing span: 26 ft 11¾ in (8.25 m)
Length overall: 23 ft 3½ in (7.10 m)
Cabin:
   Length 5 ft 5 in (1.65 m)
   Max width approx 3 ft 3¼ in (1.00 m)
   Max height approx 3 ft 11¼ in (1.20 m)
   Volume approx 53 cu ft (1.50 m³)

SIAI-MARCHETTI SF.260MX and SF.260W WARRIOR (Italy)

First flights 1969/1972

Baggage compartment volume: approx 6.36 cu ft (0.18 m³)
Max T-O weight: 2 998 lb (1 360 kg)
Max level speed at S/L: 183 knots (211 mph; 340 km/h)
Max rate of climb at S/L: 1 493 ft (455 m)/min
Service ceiling: 16 400 ft (5 000 m)
Range with max fuel: 776 nm (894 miles; 1 440 km)
Accommodation: Side-by-side adjustable seats for instructor and pupil, with third seat at rear. Baggage compartment aft of rear seat. Dual controls standard
Armament (SF.260W Warrior only): Up to 660 lb (300 kg) of stores on two underwing pylons. Typical alternative loads when carrying a crew of two include two Matra MAC AAF1 7.62 mm gun pods; two 50 kg bombs; two Matra F2 launchers, each with six 68 mm SNEB 253 rockets; two Simpres AL 9-70 launchers, each with nine 2.75 in FFAR rockets; two Simpres AL 18-50 launchers, each with eighteen 2 in SNIA ARF/8M2 rockets; or two Alkan 20AP cartridge throwers for Lacroix 74 mm explosive cartridges, flare cartridges or F.130 smoke cartridges. As a single-seater, two 120 kg bombs can be carried
Ordered by: SF.260MX: Air forces of Belgium (36 SF.260M), Philippines (32 SF.260MP), Singapore (16 SF.260MS), Thailand (12 SF.260MT), Zaïre (12 SF.260MC) and Zambia (8 SF.260MZ)
SF.260W Warrior: Philippine Air Force (16)

SIAI-MARCHETTI SM.1019 (Italy)
First flight 1969

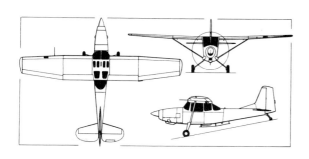

Data: Initial production version

Power plant: One Allison 250-B15G (T63) turboprop engine (317 shp)

Wing span: 36 ft 0 in (10.97 m)

Length overall (tail up): 27 ft 11½ in (8.52 m)

Cabin:
Max length approx 6 ft 6¾ in (2.00 m)
Max width approx 2 ft 0¾ in (0.63 m)
Max height approx 4 ft 1¼ in (1.25 m)
Volume 38.8 cu ft (1.10 m³)

Baggage compartment volume: 3.5 cu ft (0.1 m³)

Max payload: 1 300 lb (590 kg)

Max T-O weight: 2 800 lb (1 270 kg)

Max cruising speed at 9 845 ft (3 000 m): 135 knots (155 mph; 250 km/h)

Max rate of climb at S/L: 2 165 ft (660 m)/min

Accommodation: Pilot and one passenger (or co-pilot) seated in tandem. Dual controls optional

Armament and operational equipment: Rack installed· beneath each wing for bombs, rockets or reconnaissance cameras

Ordered by: Italian Army (100)

General-purpose helicopter

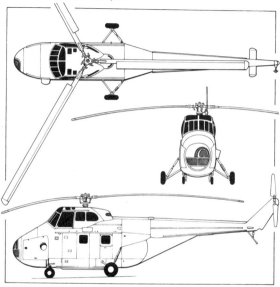

Photo and drawing: Whirlwind HAR Mk 10
Data: Westland Whirlwind Series 3
Power plant: One Bristol Siddeley Gnome H.1000 turboshaft engine (1 050 shp)
Main rotor diameter: 53 ft 0 in (16.15 m)

SIKORSKY S-55/H-19 CHICKASAW/ WESTLAND WHIRLWIND (USA/UK)
First flights 1949/1952

Length of fuselage: 44 ft 2 in (13.46 m)
Cabin:
   Length 10 ft 0 in (3.05 m)
   Max width 6 ft 0 in (1.82 m)
   Max height 5 ft 6 in (1.67 m)
   Volume 340 cu ft (9.63 m³)
Max T-O weight: 8 000 lb (3 629 kg)
Max level speed at S/L: 92 knots (106 mph; 170 km/h)
Max rate of climb at S/L: 1 200 ft (366 m)/min
Service ceiling: 10 000 ft (3 050 m)
Range with standard tanks: 260 nm (300 miles; 480 km)
Accommodation: Crew of two with dual controls, and up to 10 passengers, six stretchers or freight
Ordered by: Air forces of Argentine (6 S-55), Brazil (Air Force 5 H-19D; Navy 2 Whirlwind Srs 1 and 5 Srs 3), Chile (6 S-55T), Cuba (2 Whirlwind), Dominica (2 S-55), Ghana (7 H-19D and 3 Whirlwind Srs 3), Greece (10 UH-19D), Guatemala (3 S-55), Honduras (3 H-19), Iran (2 Whirlwind Srs 2), Japan (Army 29 H-19), Jordan (4 Whirlwind), South Korea (6 UH-19), Nigeria (1 Whirlwind Srs 3), Qatar (Security Forces 2 Whirlwind Srs 3), Spain (Navy 9 SH-19D), Taiwan (10 UH-19), Thailand (13 UH-19), Turkey (10 UH-19D), UK (Air Force 75 Whirlwind HAR. Mk 4/CC. Mk 8/HAR. Mk 10; Navy 25 HAS. Mk 7/HAR. Mk 9), USA (Air Force UH-19; Navy CH-19; Army UH-19 Chickasaw), Venezuela (10 UH-19) and Yugoslavia (20 Whirlwind Srs 2). Quantities represent approx numbers in service, not original orders

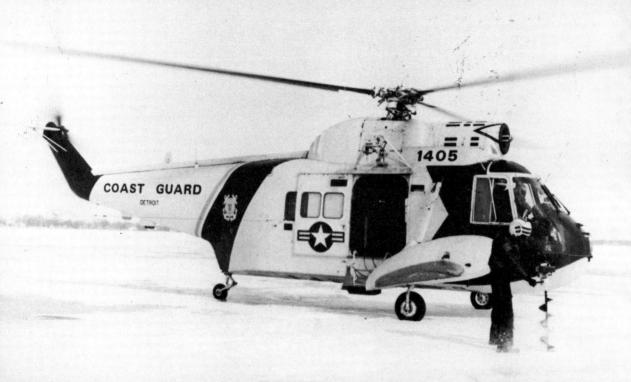

COAST GUARD

DETROIT

1405

SIKORSKY S-62/HH-52A (USA)
First flight 1958

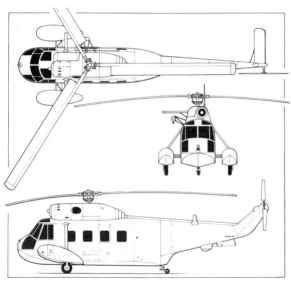

Photo and drawing: HH-52A

Data: HH-52A

Power plant: One General Electric CT58-110-1 (military T58-GE-8) turboshaft engine (1 250 shp, derated to 730 shp)

Main rotor diameter: 53 ft 0 in (16.16 m)

Length of fuselage: 44 ft 6½ in (13.58 m)

Cabin, excl flight deck:
Length 14 ft 0 in (4.27 m)
Max width 5 ft 4 in (1.62 m)
Max height 6 ft 0 in (1.83 m)
Volume 440 cu ft (12.45 m³)

Baggage hold (fwd, stbd side of cabin): 44 cu ft (1.25 m³)

Max useful load: 3 017 lb (1 368 kg)

Max T-O weight: 8 100 lb (3 674 kg)

Max overload T-O weight (sling load): 8 300 lb (3 765 kg)

Max level speed at S/L: 95 knots (109 mph; 175 km/h)

Max rate of climb at S/L: 1 080 ft (329 m)/min

Service ceiling: 11 200 ft (3 410 m)

Range with main and aft tanks, 10% reserve: 412 nm (474 miles; 763 km)

Accommodation: Crew of two or three, and up to 12 passengers

Ordered by: Air forces of India (2 S-62), Japan (8 S-62), Philippines (2 S-62), Thailand (Police Dept 2 S-62) and USA (Coast Guard 99 HH-52A)

Armed basic trainer and light strike aircraft

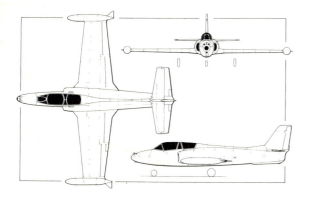

SOKO G2-A GALEB (Yugoslavia)
First flight 1961

Power plant: One Rolls-Royce Bristol Viper 11 Mk 22-6
turbojet engine (2 500 lb; 1 134 kg st)
Wing span over tip-tanks: 38 ft 1½ in (11.62 m)
Length overall: 33 ft 11 in (10.34 m)
Max T-O weight:
trainer, clean 7 438 lb (3 374 kg)
strike version 9 210 lb (4 178 kg)
Max level speed at 20 350 ft (6 200 m): 438 knots
(505 mph; 812 km/h)
Max rate of climb at S/L: 4 500 ft (1 370 m)/min
Service ceiling: 39 375 ft (12 000 m)
Max range at 29 520 ft (9 000 m), with tip-tanks full:
669 nm (770 miles; 1 240 km)
Accommodation: Crew of two in tandem on Folland Type
1-B fully-automatic lightweight ejection seats
Armament: Two 0.50 in machine-guns in nose (with 80
rds/gun); underwing pylons for two 50 kg or 100 kg
bombs and four 57 mm rockets or two 127 mm rockets
Ordered by: Air forces of Yugoslavia (60) and Zambia (2)

Medium-range troop and freight transport

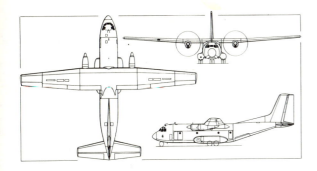

Photo: Transall C-160 D
Data: C-160 D/F
Power plant: Two Rolls-Royce Tyne RTy.20 Mk 22 turboprop engines (each 6 100 ehp)
Wing span: 131 ft 3 in (40.00 m)
Length overall: 106 ft 3½ in (32.40 m)
Cabin, excluding flight deck and ramp:
    Length 44 ft 4 in (13.51 m)
    Max width 10 ft 3½ in (3.15 m)
    Max height 9 ft 8½ in (2.98 m)
    Volume 4 072 cu ft (115.3 m³)

Cabin, including ramp:
    Length 56 ft 6 in (17.21 m)
    Volume 4 940 cu ft (139.9 m³)
Max payload: 35 270 lb (16 000 kg)
Max T-O weight: 112 440 lb (51 000 kg)
Max level speed at 14 760 ft (4 500 m), at AUW of 90 390 lb (41 000 kg): 289 knots (333 mph; 536 km/h)
Max rate of climb at S/L at max T-O weight: 1 440 ft (440 m)/min
Service ceiling at AUW of 99 225 lb (45 000 kg): 27 900 ft (8 500 m)
Range with 17 640 lb (8 000 kg) payload, 10% fuel reserves and allowance for 30 min at 13 125 ft (4 000 m): 2 459 nm (2 832 miles; 4 558 km)
Range with max payload, reserves as above: 634 nm (730 miles; 1 175 km)
Accommodation: Flight crew of four. Typical payloads include 93 troops or 61-81 fully-equipped paratroops; 62 stretchers and four attendants; armoured vehicles, tanks and tractors; one empty five-ton truck and crew; two empty three-ton trucks and crews; or three jeeps with partially-loaded trailers and crews. Individual loads of up to 17 640 lb (8 000 kg) can be air-dropped
Ordered by: France (Air Force 50 C-160 F), German Federal Republic (Air Force 110 C-160 D, of which 20 since transferred to Turkish Air Force) and South Africa (Air Force 9 C-160 Z)

General utility and ambulance aircraft

UTVA-60 and UTVA-66 (Yugoslavia)
First flights 1961(?) / 1967(?)

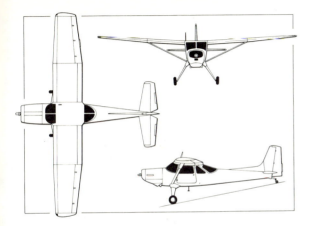

Photo and drawing: UTVA-66

Data: UTVA-66
Power plant: One Lycoming GSO-480-B1J6 six-cylinder piston engine (270 hp)
Wing span: 37 ft 5 in (11.40 m)
Length overall: 27 ft 6 in (8.38 m)
Cabin:
Length 4 ft 11 in (1.50 m)
Width 3 ft 5 in (1.05 m)
Height 3 ft 11 in (1.20 m)
Max T-O weight: 4 000 lb (1 814 kg)
Max level speed at optimum height: 135 knots (155 mph; 250 km/h)
Max rate of climb at S/L: 885 ft (270 m)/min
Service ceiling: 22 000 ft (6 700 m)
Range with standard fuel: 404 nm (466 miles; 750 km)
Accommodation: Pilot and three passengers; or pilot, two stretchers and attendant in ambulance version
Ordered by: Yugoslav Air Force

Primary and basic trainer (TS-11) and armament trainer (Iskra 100)

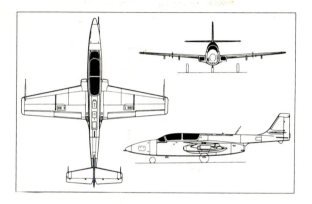

Photo and drawing: Iskra 100

WSK-MIELEC TS-11 ISKRA (Poland)
First flight 1960

Data: Trainer version
Power plant: One ISO-3 turbojet engine (2 205 lb; 1 000 kg st)
Wing span: 33 ft 0¼ in (10.07 m)
Length overall: 36 ft 10¾ in (11.25 m)
Normal T-O weight: 8 068 lb (3 660 kg)
Max T-O weight: 8 377 lb (3 800 kg)
Max level speed at 16 400 ft (5 000 m), at normal T-O weight: 388 knots (447 mph; 720 km/h)
Max rate of climb at S/L, normal T-O weight: 3 150 ft (960 m)/min
Service ceiling, normal T-O weight: 41 000 ft (12 500 m)
Range with max fuel, normal T-O weight: 787 nm (907 miles; 1 460 km)
Accommodation: Crew of two in tandem on lightweight ejection seats
Armament (Iskra 100 only): Forward-firing 23 mm cannon in nose on starboard side, with gun camera. Four attachments for a variety of underwing stores, including bombs of up to 110 lb (50 kg) and rockets
Ordered by: Polish Air Force (several hundred)

NATO Code Name *Hoplite*
General-purpose light helicopter

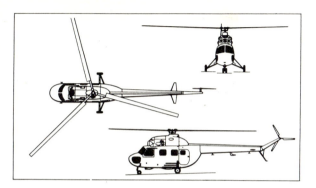

Power plant: Two Isotov GTD-350 turboshaft engines (each 437 shp)
Main rotor diameter: 47 ft 6¾ in (14.50 m)
Length of fuselage: 37 ft 4¾ in (11.40 m)
Cabin:
  Length, excl flight deck 7 ft 5½ in (2.27 m)
  Mean width 3 ft 11¼ in (1.20 m)
  Mean height 4 ft 7 in (1.40 m)
Max payload, excl pilot, oil and fuel (external sling load): 1 763 lb (800 kg)
Max T-O weight (normal): 7 826 lb (3 550 kg)
Max level speed at 1 640 ft (500 m): 113 knots (130 mph; 210 km/h)
Max rate of climb at S/L: 885 ft (270 m)/min
Service ceiling: 13 755 ft (4 200 m)
Range at 1 640 ft (500 m) with max fuel, 30 min reserve: 313 nm (360 miles; 580 km)
Range at 1 640 ft (500 m) with max payload, 5% fuel reserve: 91 nm (105 miles; 170 km)
Accommodation: Normal accommodation for pilot and up to eight passengers. All cabin seats removable for carrying 1 543 lb (700 kg) of internal freight. Ambulance version can carry four stretchers and a medical attendant. Side-by-side front seats and dual controls in pilot training version
Ordered by: Air forces of Poland, USSR and other east European countries

NATO Code Name *Max*
Primary trainer

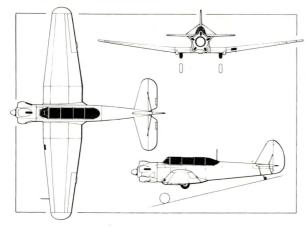

Photo and drawing: Yak-18

YAKOVLEV Yak-18 (USSR)
First flight 1946

Data: Yak-18A
Power plant: One Ivchenko AI-14R nine-cylinder radial piston engine (260 hp)
Wing span: 34 ft 9¼ in (10.60 m)
Length overall: 27 ft 11¾ in (8.53 m)
Max T-O weight: 2 901 lb (1 316 kg)
Max level speed: 140 knots (162 mph; 260 km/h)
Max rate of climb at S/L: 1 043 ft (318 m)/min
Service ceiling: 16 600 ft (5 060 m)
Range with max fuel: 405 nm (465 miles; 750 km)
Accommodation: Two seats in tandem
Ordered by: Air forces of Afghanistan, Albania, Bulgaria, China, Egypt, German Democratic Republic, Hungary, North Korea, Mali, Mongolia and USSR

NATO Code Name *Codling*
Short-range personnel transport

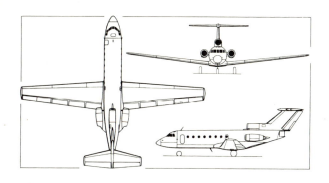

Power plant: Three Ivchenko AI-25 turbofan engines (each 3 300 lb; 1 500 kg st)
Wing span: 82 ft 0¼ in (25.00 m)
Length overall: 66 ft 9½ in (20.36 m)
Cabin:
    Length 23 ft 2½ in (7.07 m)
    Max width 7 ft 0¾ in (2.15 m)
    Max height 6 ft 0¾ in (1.85 m)
Max payload: 6 000 lb (2 720 kg)
Max T-O weight: 35 275 lb (16 000 kg)
Max level speed at S/L: 324 knots (373 mph; 600 km/h) IAS
Max rate of climb at S/L: 1 575 ft (480 m)/min
Max range at 254 knots (292 mph; 470 km/h) at 31 500 ft (8 000 m), no reserve: 1 080 nm (1 240 miles; 2 000 km)
Accommodation: Flight crew of two or three and up to 32 passengers. Baggage compartment aft of main cabin
Ordered by: Yugoslav Air Force (3 or more); likely also to be in service with Soviet Air Force

INDEX

INDEX

PHOTOGRAPHS:

Air Portraits 138, 146
APN 32, 152
Aviation Week and Space Technology 28
M J Axe 170
D Balaguer 140
C C Brunckhorst 174
Canadian Forces 74, 80, 120, 166
Paul R Duffy 118
Martin Fricke 208
J M G Gradidge 60, 150
D J Holford 30
Denis Hughes 88, 192, 202, 214
Indian Navy 34
Italian Air Ministry 200
Duane A Kasulka 116
R L Lawson 162
G MacAdie 122
P R March 54, 154, 176, 190
T Matsuzaki 142, 156, 160, 222
Ministère des Armées "Air", Paris 168
Ministry of Defence, London 38, 128
NASA 240
Ronaldo S Olive 18, 24, 100
S P Peltz 62, 76, 96, 104, 206, 228
Alex Reinhard 106
Royal Netherlands Air Force 16, 78

Brian M Service 36, 84, 98, 148, 158, 164
Spanish Air Force 194, 212
Max Stevens 14
Y Takahashi 184
Tass 26
Norman E Taylor 70, 94
John Wegg 254
M D West 48
Gordon S Williams 102, 178

DRAWINGS:

Michael A Badrocke 17, 19, 25, 59, 77, 103, 107, 113, 115, 123, 137, 143, 145, 155, 169, 173, 175, 177, 179, 183, 187, 189, 191, 193, 201, 203, 205, 209, 219, 233, 235, 239, 241, 243, 247, 253

Roy J Grainge 37, 41, 43, 45, 47, 49, 55, 57, 63, 65, 67, 69, 71, 79, 81, 89, 93, 95, 97, 99, 105, 111, 117, 121, 125, 133, 135, 147, 151, 153, 161, 165, 167, 195, 197, 211, 213, 215, 221, 223

Pilot Press 7, 9, 11, 13, 15, 21, 23, 27, 29, 31, 33, 35, 39, 51, 53, 61, 73, 75, 83, 85, 87, 91, 101, 109, 119, 127, 129, 131, 139, 141, 149, 157, 159, 163, 171, 181, 185, 199, 207, 217, 225, 227, 229, 231, 237, 245, 249, 251, 255